KV-636-021

A GUIDE TO STUDIES
ON THE
CHANSON DE ROLAND

by

JOSEPH J. DUGGAN

Grant & Cutler Ltd
1976

© Grant & Cutler Ltd
1976

ISBN 0 7293 0018 X

QUEEN MARY
COLLEGE
LIBRARY

I.S.B.N. 84-399-6351-3

DEPÓSITO LEGAL: v. 457 - 1977

Printed in Spain by Artes Gráficas Soler, S.A., Valencia

for

GRANT & CUTLER LTD
11, BUCKINGHAM STREET, LONDON, W.C.2

QMC ⠀⠀⠀⠀⠀ 650013 9

a30213 0065001396

DATE DUE FOR RETURN

RESEARCH BIBLIOGRAPHIES & CHECKLISTS

DATE DUE FOR RETURN

30. OCT 87.

20. OCT 93

17 JAN 2008

WITHDRAWN
FROM STOCK
QMUL LIBRARY

RESEARCH BIBLIOGRAPHIES & CHECKLISTS

RCB

General editors

A. D. Deyermond, J. R. Little and J. E. Varey

Editors' Preface

* * *

The aim of this series is to provide research students and scholars with bibliographical information on aspects of Western European literature from the Middle Ages to the present day, in a convenient and accessible form. We hope to supplement, not to supplant, existing material. Single authors, periods or topics will be chosen for treatment wherever a gap needs to be filled and an authoritative scholar is prepared to fill it. Compilers will choose the form appropriate to each subject, ranging from the unannotated checklist to the selective critical bibliography; full descriptive bibliography is not, however, envisaged. Supplements will be issued, when appropriate, to keep the bibliographies up to date.

CONTENTS

Contents

PREFACE

This bibliography gives an account of works published in the years 1955 through 1974 on the *Chanson de Roland* and materials closely related to its study. For the period preceding 1955, items of overriding critical or historical significance have been included, as well as those which provide extensive bibliographies or outstanding surveys of the subjects to which they are devoted. I have chosen 1955 as a watershed for several reasons. *Roland* studies have not been the same since Jean Rychner published in that year his descriptive work on the jongleur's art, identifying it with the craft of the improvising singer. A measure of his book's success is the manner in which its conclusions dominated the Colloquium held at Liège in 1957 on the literary technique of the *chanson de geste*. Pierre Le Gentil's comprehensive treatment of the poem also appeared in 1955. While historical problems still attract considerable activity, and rightly so, students of the *Roland* have in the last two decades focussed their critical powers increasingly upon the poem's aesthetic qualities. In addition, the congresses of the Société Rencesvals, the first of which was held at Pamplona and Roncesvalles in 1956, have provided an opportunity for scholarly dialogue which was not regularly available until then.

I have attempted to serve the needs of both students and experienced researchers. The latter are asked to forgive me for calling attention to many elementary but important facts which are meant for the consumption of those who have only lately taken up the study of the poem. Since the last comprehensive bibliography on the subject is already nearly seventy years old, I have preferred the risk of saying too much to that of omitting essential information.

Summaries and evaluative comments are given for the works to which I have had access, with the exception of unpublished theses, and reviews are indicated for items which have appeared since 1955. Review-articles are normally treated as reviews, rather than listed independently. In addition to those abbreviations which are common in bibliographical references, I have employed the following:

Ch	Charlemagne	*CR*	*Chanson de Roland*
O	Oxford MS	R	Roland

My work has been lightened by others, notably the authors —too often anonymous— of the bibliographies listed in Chapter I. I am particularly indebted as well to Margery Fanelli, Marcia Goodman, Jeannot Nyles, and Donald G. Williams of the Interlibrary Borrowing Service of the University of California, Berkeley, from whose search few books or periodicals, however obscure, have escaped. Thanks are due to my research assistants Michael Harney, Jeffrey Peck, Eileen Maloy, Evalin Shelly, and Jean Blacker-Knight, and to Richard Lock and Eric Rutledge, who tracked down the Japanese entries. Grants from the Committee on Research and the Humanities Research Institute of the University of California, Berkeley, gave me the material means and the freedom from teaching and administrative chores which I needed to complete the project. Ian Short, Alan Deyermond, and Roger Little went over the manuscript with meticulous care, and gave me many valuable suggestions. To all those involved, I express my gratitude. Any errors which remain despite their efforts are, of course, my own.

Berkeley, June 1975   Joseph J. Duggan

ABBREVIATIONS

AEM	*Anuario de Estudios Medievales*
AMi	*Annales du Midi*
Archiv	*Archiv für das Studium der Neueren Sprachen und Literaturen*
AUMLA	*Journal of the Australasian Universities Language and Literature Association*
BBF	*Bulletin des Bibliothèques de France*
BBSR	*Bulletin Bibliographique de la Société Rencesvals*
BGDSL	*Beiträge zur Geschichte der Deutschen Sprache und Literatur*
BH	*Bulletin Hispanique*
BHR	*Bibliothèque d'Humanisme et Renaissance*
BHS	*Bulletin of Hispanic Studies*
BRABLB	*Boletin de la Real Academia de Buenas Letras de Barcelona*
BRAE	*Boletin de la Real Academia Española*
CCM	*Cahiers de Civilisation Médiévale*
CH	*Computers and the Humanities*
CHA	*Cuadernos Hispanoamericanos*
CLS	*Comparative Literature Studies*
CN	*Cultura Neolatina*
Coloquios de Roncesvalles	*Coloquios de Roncesvalles.* (Publicaciones de la Facultad de Filosofía y Letras de la Univ. de Zaragoza, 2a serie, III) Saragossa: Institución Príncipe de Viana, 1956
Congrès d'Aix	Société Rencesvals. VIᵉ Congrès International (Aix-en-Provence, 29 août - 4 septembre, 1973). Aix-en-Provence: Univ. de Provence, 1974
La coscienza letteraria	Battaglia, Salvatore. *La coscienza letteraria del medioevo.* (Collana di testi e di critica, II) Naples: Liguori, 1965

13

CRAIBL	*Comptes-rendus de l'Académie des Inscriptions et Belles Lettres*
DA	*Dissertation Abstracts*
DAI	*Dissertation Abstracts International*
EC	*Etudes Critiques*
ECr	*L'Esprit Créateur*
Ewert Studies	*Studies in Medieval French Presented to Alfred Ewert in Honour of his Seventieth Birthday.* Oxford: Clarendon Press, 1961
Festschrift Mönch	*Aus der französischen Kultur- und Geistesgeschichte. Festschrift zum 65. Geburtstag von Walter Mönch.* Edited by Werner Dierlamm and Wolfgang Drost. Heidelberg: Kerle, 1971
Festschrift Rheinfelder	*Medium Aevum Romanicum. Festschrift für Hans Rheinfelder.* Edited by Heinrich Bihler and Alfred Noyer-Weidner. Munich: Hueber, 1963
FMLS	*Forum for Modern Language Studies*
FR	*Filologia Romanza*
FrR	*French Review*
FS	*French Studies*
Gesammelte Aufsätze	Curtius, Ernst Robert. *Gesammelte Aufsätze zur romanischen Philologie.* Berne: Francke, 1960
GRM	*Germanisch-Romanische Monatsschrift*, Neue Folge
Heidelberg Colloquium	*Société Rencesvals. IVᵉ Congrès international. Heidelberg, 29 août - 2 septembre 1967. Actes et mémoires.* (Studia Romanica, XIV) Heidelberg: Winter, 1969
Homenaje a Dámaso Alonso	*Studia Philologica. Homenaje ofrecido a Dámaso Alonso por sus amigos y discípulos con ocasión de su 60.º aniversario.* 3 vols, Madrid: Gredos, 1960-3
Hommage à Maurice Delbouille	*Hommage au professeur Maurice Delbouille.* Edited by Jeanne Wathelet-Willem. (*Marche Romane*, special issue) Liège: Cahiers de l'Association des Romanistes de l'Université de Liège, 1973
IL	*L'Information Littéraire*
Langue et littérature	*Langue et littérature. Actes du VIIIᵉ Congrès de la Fédération Internationale des Langues et Littératures Modernes.* (Bibliothèque de la Faculté de Philosophie et Lettres de l'Université de Liège,

	CLXI) Paris: Les Belles Lettres, 1961
LI	*Lettere Italiane*
LR	*Les Lettres Romanes*
MA	*Le Moyen Age*
MAe	*Medium Aevum*
Mélanges Boutière	*Mélanges de philologie romane dédiés à la mémoire de Jean Boutière (1899-1967).* Edited by Irénée Cluzel and François Pirot. 2 vols, Liège: Soledo, 1971
Mélanges Crozet	*Mélanges offerts à René Crozet à l'occasion de son soixante-dixième anniversaire.* Edited by Pierre Gallais and Yves-Jean Riou. 2 vols, Poitiers: Société d'Etudes Médiévales, 1966
Mélanges Delbouille	*Mélanges de linguistique romane et de philologie médiévale offerts à M. Maurice Delbouille. I. Linguistique romane. II. Philologie médiévale.* Gembloux: Duculot, 1964
Mélanges Frank	*Mélanges de linguistique et de littérature romanes à la mémoire d'István Frank.* (Annales Universitatis Saraviensis, VI) Saarbrucken: Univ. des Saarlandes, 1957
Mélanges Frappier	*Mélanges de langue et de littérature du moyen âge et de la Renaissance offerts à Jean Frappier.* 2 vols (PRF, CXII) Geneva: Droz, 1970
Mélanges Le Gentil	*Mélanges de langue et de littérature médiévales offerts à Pierre Le Gentil, par ses collègues, ses élèves et ses amis.* Paris: SEDES, 1973
Mélanges Lejeune	*Mélanges offerts à Rita Lejeune.* 2 vols, Gembloux: Duculot, 1969
Mélanges Lombard	*Mélanges de philologie offerts à Alf Lombard à l'occasion de son soixante-cinquième anniversaire par ses collègues et amis.* (Etudes Romanes de Lund, XVIII) Lund: Gleerup, 1969
MLJ	*Modern Language Journal*
MLN	*Modern Language Notes*
MLQ	*Modern Language Quarterly*
MLR	*Modern Language Review*
MR	*Marche Romane*
NC	*La Nouvelle Clio*

Nuevos estudios	Richthofen, Erich von. *Nuevos estudios épicos medievales.* (Biblioteca Románica Hispánica, II. Estudios y Ensayos, CXXXVIII) Madrid: Gredos, 1970
PMLA	*Publications of the Modern Language Association of America*
PRF	Publications Romanes et Françaises
La poesia epica	*La poesia epica e la sua formazione. Atti del Convegno internazionale. Roma, 28 marzo - 3 aprile 1969.* (Accademia Nazionale dei Lincei, Anno 367. Problemi Attuali di Scienza e di Cultura, CXXXIX) Rome, 1970
RBPH	*Revue Belge de Philologie et d'Histoire*
RF	*Romanische Forschungen*
RFE	*Revista de Filología Española*
RHE	*Revue d'Histoire Ecclésiastique*
RIO	*Revue Internationale d'Onomastique*
RJ	*Romanistisches Jahrbuch*
RLiR	*Revue de Linguistique Romane*
RLR	*Revue des Langues Romanes*
RN	*Romance Notes*
Rolandiana et Oliveriana	Aebischer, Paul. *Rolandiana et Oliveriana. Recueil d'études sur les chansons de geste.* (PRF, XCII) Geneva: Droz, 1967
RPh	*Romance Philology*
RR	*Romanic Review*
RSH	*Revue Suisse d'Histoire*
SATF	Société des Anciens Textes Français
SF	*Studi Francesi*
SM	*Studi Medievali,* 3rd series
SMV	*Studi Mediolatini e Volgari*
SRÜ	Sammlung Romanischer Übungstexte
Studi Monteverdi	*Studi in onore di Angelo Monteverdi.* 2 vols, Modena: Società Tipografica Editrice Modenese, 1959
Studi rolandiani	Pellegrini, Silvio. *Studi rolandiani e trobadorici.* (Biblioteca di Filologia Romanza, VIII) Bari: Adriatica, 1964
Studi Siciliano	*Studi in onore di Italo Siciliano.* (Biblioteca

	dell'*Archivum Romanicum*, serie I, vol. LXXXVI) 2 vols, Firenze: Olschki, 1966
La Technique littéraire	*La Technique littéraire des chansons de geste: Actes du Colloque de Liège (septembre 1957).* (Publications de la Faculté de Philosophie et Lettres de l'Univ. de Liège, CL) Paris: Les Belles Lettres, 1959
TLL	*Travaux de Linguistique et de Littérature*
TLS	*Times Literary Supplement*
VIII Congresso	*VIII Congresso Internazionale di Studi Romanzi. Firenze, 3 - 8 aprile 1956. Atti.* Florence: Sansoni, 1960
Xe Congrès	*Xe Congrès International de linguistique et de philologie romanes. Actes.* Edited by Georges Straka. (Actes et Colloques, IV) Paris: Klincksieck, 1965
XI Congreso	*XI Congreso Internacional de Lingüística y Filología Románicas. Actas.* 4 vols. Edited by Antonio Quilis with Ramón B. Carril and Margarita Cantarero. (*RFE*, anejo LXXXVI) Madrid, 1968
XII-lea Congres	*Actele celui de-al XII-lea Congres internaţional lingvistică şi filologie romanică.* 2 vols. Edited by Alexandru Rosetti. Bucarest: Editura Academiei Republicii Socialiste România, 1970-1.
ZFSL	*Zeitschrift für Französische Sprache und Literatur*
ZRP	*Zeitschrift für Romanische Philologie*
ZSRG	*Zeitschrift der Savigny-Stiftung für Rechtsgeschichte,* Germanistische Abteilung
Zur romanischen Literatur-geschichte	Becker, Philipp August. *Zur romanischen Literaturgeschichte: Ausgewählte Studien und Aufsätze.* Edited by Martha Ellen Becker. Munich: Francke, 1967

I
BIBLIOGRAPHIES AND REVIEWS OF RESEARCH

An adequate listing of current publications on the *CR* can be obtained only by recourse to a variety of bibliographical tools, no one of which is exhaustive. The most thorough sources available are:

1   Klapp, Otto. *Bibliographie der französischen Literaturwissenschaft.* Frankfurt am Main: Klostermann, 1960- .
The first volume includes works published from 1956.

2   *Zeitschrift für Romanische Philologie. Bibliographie.* 1875-1960. *Romanische Bibliographie.* 1961- .
Appears as a supplement to the journal. Fairly complete.

Other useful general serial bibliographies are:

3   *Publications of the Modern Language Association of America. Bibliography.* New York: Modern Language Association. 1921- .
International from 1955. Neither thorough nor always accurate.

3A   *Bulletin Signalétique. Section 523 : Histoire et Science de la Littérature.* Centre de Documentation du Centre National de la Recherche Scientifique. 1947- .
Summarizes articles. Incomplete but useful. Before vol. XXIII (1969), the literary section appeared as *Bulletin Signalétique 23.*

4   Rancœur, René. *Bibliographie de la littérature française du moyen âge à nos jours.* Paris: Colin, 1966- .

5   *The Year's Work in Modern Language Studies.* London: Modern Humanities Research Association, 1931- .
Selective, with a running commentary.

6   *Studi Francesi.* I (1957)- .
The "Rassegna bibliografica" reviews articles as well as books.

Three serial bibliographies of medieval studies sometimes include items missed by the literary compilations:

7   *Cahiers de Civilisation Médiévale.* I (1958)- . "Bibliographie."
Difficult to use, since book reviews are listed separately from articles and

books. From 1969 the bibliography is issued annually as a fifth fascicle of the journal.

8   *International Guide to Medieval Studies: A Quarterly Index to Periodical Literature.* I (1961-2)- . Darien, Connecticut: American Bibliographic Service.
Indexes articles and book reviews. Not comprehensive.

9   *International Medieval Bibliography.* 1967- . Directed by P. H. Sawyer. Edited by Patricia Neal. Univ. of Leeds.
Indexes articles, arranged by subject.

Two more specialized bibliographies cover the period up to 1960:

10   Holmes, Urban T., Jr., ed. *The Mediaeval Period.* Vol. I of *A Critical Bibliography of French Literature*, edited by David C. Cabeen. Syracuse: Syracuse Univ. Press, 1947. Enlarged edition, 1952.
Chapter 6, "Origins of the Epic; Major Cycles of the Twelfth Century," is by Charles A. Knudson. Selective.

11   Bossuat, Robert. *Manuel bibliographique de la littérature française du moyen âge.* (Bibliothèque Elzévirienne. Nouvelle Série. Etudes et Documents) Melun: Librairie d'Argences, 1951. *Supplément (1949-53).* In collaboration with Jacques Monfrin. Paris: Librairie d'Argences, 1955. *Second supplément (1954-60).* Paris: Librairie d'Argences, 1961.

Two bibliographies of the Société Rencesvals provide information on epic studies:

12   *Bulletin bibliographique de la Société Rencesvals.* Paris: Nizet, 1958- . Vols I (1958), II (1960), III (1963), IV (1967), V (1970), VI (1971), VII (1972).
Although this bibliography is of prime importance for students of the Romance epic, it is incomplete and organized in a way which makes it cumbersome to use, recently according to the countries in which items were published. Summaries are provided.

13   Société Rencesvals, American-Canadian Branch. "Bibliographical Note."
Vols I through VII (1966-72), and vol. VIII, nos 1 and 2 (1973) were issued in mimeographed form. Thereafter the note is found in *Olifant*, which also publishes abstracts of selected articles.

Bibliographies of the *CR* aspiring to completeness are only available for the period up to 1906:

14 Bauquier, Joseph. *Bibliographie de la CR.* Heilbronn: Henninger, 1877.

15 Seelmann, Emil. *Bibliographie des altfranzösischen Rolandsliedes, mit Berücksichtigung nahestehender Sprach- und Litteraturdenkmale.* Wiesbaden: Sändig, 1969. Reprint of the original, published in 1888.

16 Gautier, Léon. "La *CR.*" *Bibliographie des chansons de geste.* Paris: Welter, 1897. Pp. 170- 99. Reprint with additions in James Geddes, tr. *La CR: A Modern French Translation.* New York: Macmillan, 1906. Pp. xci-clx.

A handy critical survey of selected scholarship on the *CR* is included in:

17 Knudson, Charles A., and Jean Misrahi. "French Medieval Literature." *The Medieval Literature of Western Europe: A Review of Research,* edited by John H. Fisher. New York: New York Univ. Press, 1966.

For research on *O* carried out in the early 1950s, see:

18 Junker, Albert. "Stand der Forschung zum *Rolandslied.*" *GRM*, VI (1956), 97-144.
   rev: Aebischer, *RBPH*, XXXVI (1958), 170-1; Whitehead, *FS*, XII (1958), 262-3.

A number of reviews of scholarship were published as a result of the neotraditionalist-individualist controversy stirred up by the publication of Ramón Menéndez Pidal's *magnum opus* (541):

19 Roussel, Henri. "Où en sont les études sur les chansons de geste françaises? "*IL*, XI (1959), 47-54. Repr. in *The Present State of French Studies: A Collection of Research Reviews,* edited by Charles B. Osburn. Metuchen, New Jersey: Scarecrow Press, 1971. Pp. 33-67.

20 Pasero, Niccolò. "La *CR* e i problemi dell'epica francese." *Il Verri*, V, no. 1 (February 1961), pp. 129-48.

21 Junker, Albert. "Von der Schönheit des *Rolandsliedes (O)* im Spiegel neuester Forschung." *Festschrift Rheinfelder*, pp. 186-99.
   Deals with aesthetic rather than historical topics. rev: Müller, *ZFSL*, LXXV (1965), 81-2.

22 Renzi, Lorenzo. "Gli ultimi studi sulla *CR* e la redazione

franco-veneta (ms. *V4*)." *LI*, XVI (1964), 324-39.
Compares Menéndez Pidal's ideas with those of Rosellini (89).

23 Christmann, Hans Helmut. "Neuere Arbeiten zum *Rolandslied*." *RJ*, XVI (1965), 49-60.
Discusses especially the neotraditionalist-individualist controversy, but also other work which concentrates on the poem itself.

24 Knudson, Charles A. "Quel terrain faut-il céder au néo-traditionalisme? Le cas de la *CR*." *BRABLB*, XXXI (1965-6), 119-31.
Only grants possible concessions on the question of oral transmission.

25 Van Emden, Wolfgang Georg. "*La bataille est aduree endementres*: Traditionalism and Individualism in *Chanson-de-Geste* Studies." *Nottingham Medieval Studies*, XIII (1969), 3-26.
Suggests, by way of conciliation, that the *chanson de geste* would have been sung and composed orally to at least the end of the thirteenth c., but is also, in its extant form, a literary genre.

26 Müller, Franz Walter. *Don Ramón Menéndez Pidal und die Rolandsliedforschung.* (Sitzungsberichte der Wissenschaftlichen Gesellschaft an der Johann Wolfgang Goethe-Univ., Frankfurt am Main, IX [1970], pp. 129-67) Wiesbaden: Steiner Verlag, 1971.

27 Kloocke, Kurt. *Bédiers Theorie über den Ursprung der Chansons de Geste und die daran anschliessende Diskussion zwischen 1908 und 1968.* (Göppinger Akademische Beiträge, XXXIII-IV) Göppingen: Kümmerle, 1972.
Concludes that Bédier's individualist theory is no longer tenable. Bibliography, pp. 505-43.

II
COMPREHENSIVE STUDIES

The indispensable handbook, even though many of its theoretical conclusions are no longer acceptable, continues to be:

28 Bédier, Joseph. *La CR commentée*. Paris: Piazza [1927]. Repr. 1968.

A complement to Bédier's ed., this volume is sometimes referred to as the *Commentaires*. It treats questions of origins, language, versification, textual criticism, and interpretation. The version found in *O* is dated 1098-1100, and is defended as *précellent* over all other texts. Lucien Foulet's complete Glossary is on pp. 321-522.

The broadest literary treatment, including considerations of both aesthetic criticism and literary history, is:

29 Le Gentil, Pierre. *La Chanson de Roland*. (Connaissance des Lettres, XLIII) Paris: Hatier-Boivin, 1955. Second ed., revised and updated, 1967. English tr. by Frances F. Beer, Cambridge, Mass.: Harvard Univ. Press, 1969.

The bulk of this study is devoted to literary analysis: composition, unity, meaning, characterization, and style. The text, the historical events, authorship, the date, and the state of the controversy over origins are also treated. P.L.G. takes a fairly moderate stance on the interpretation of facts, and sees the *CR* as a masterpiece of narrative construction. The best comprehensive literary analysis available. rev: original ed.: Cremonesi, *CN*, XV (1955), 153; Bourciez, *RLR*, LXXII (1956), 289-90; Peckham, *RR*, XLVII (1956), 117-21; Lausberg, *Archiv*, CXCIII (1956), 83; Frank, *RPh*, X (1956-7), 284; Junker, *ZRP*, LXXIV (1958), 309-11; English tr.: Dougherty, *FrR*, XLIII (1969-70), 197-9; Nelson, *ECr*, X (1970), 157-8; Rickard, *MAe*, XXXIX (1970), 47-9; Whitehead, *FS*, XXV (1971), 442.

Still of interest is:

30 Faral, Edmond. *La Chanson de Roland: Etude et analyse*. (Les Chefs-d'œuvre de la Littérature Expliqués) Paris: Mellottée, 1934.

The *CR* as a work of art. Bédier's theory of origins is defended. The poem was created by a great individual in the late eleventh c. Bibliography, pp. 322-30.

Other general treatments of a less ambitious nature:

31 Battaglia, Salvatore. *L'epica francese: La CR e il ciclo di Guillaume d'Orange.* Naples: Pironti [1956].

32 ——.*Introduzione alla filologia romanza e la CR.* Naples: Liguori, 1967.

Treats French phonology. Extracts from *O* with tr. Essays on the problem of transmission by jongleurs and on R and Oliver.

33 Spina, Giuseppe. *Le geste di Spagna: Saggio critico sulla CR.* Naples: L'Arte Tipografico, 1968.

34 Vance, Eugene. *Reading the Song of Roland.* (Landmarks in Literature) Englewood Cliffs, New Jersey: Prentice Publishing Co., 1970.

A good introduction for students. Problems of language, the heroic society, literary conventions. Develops the idea of the "extended formula" in an analysis of the poem's language and structure. rev: Brault, *FrR*, XLIV (1970-1), 628-9; Flinn, *Univ. of Toronto Quarterly*, XL (1970-1), 335-7; Nichols, *Speculum*, XLVII (1972), 561-3; Folkart, *SF*, XVI (1972), 433; Delbouille, *CCM*, XVII (1974), 183-4.

35 Dufournet, Jean. *Cours sur la CR.* (Les Cours de Sorbonne) Paris: Centre de Documentation Universitaire, 1972.

Historical questions, textual problems, interesting and difficult passages, aspects of medieval civilization, characterization. Heavy emphasis on previous research. rev: Brault, *CCM,* XVII (1974), 165-6.

For the *CR* within its genre:

36 Riquer, Martín de. *Les Chansons de geste françaises.* Second, revised ed., tr. by Irénée-Marcel Cluzel. Paris: Nizet, 1957. Originally published as *Los cantares de gesta franceses: Sus problemas, su relación con España.* Madrid: Gredos, 1952.

The only modern survey of the genre, this work devotes 109 pp. to the *CR*, treating the historical events, the sources, the origins and transmission of the legend, the MSS and foreign versions, the date (1087-95) of the version found in *O*, the style, the author, and the literary fortunes of the legend in Spain. M. de R. supports Li Gotti's hypothesis that the author was Turoldus of Peterborough. A possible *terminus a quo* for the version of *O* is provided by the mention of Saracen battle drums, which were first used in Spain at the Battle of Zalaca, 1086. rev: Roques, *Romania*, LXXIX (1958), 553.

See also 455.

THE TEXTS

The title *Chanson de Roland* is itself ambiguous and does not in fact correspond to medieval practice:

37　Aebischer, Paul. "Le Titre originaire de la *CR*." *Studi Monteverdi*, pp. 33-47. Repr. in *Rolandiana et Oliveriana*, pp. 177-90.

> From the evidence of the MSS, the most accurate title would be *Roncevaux* or *Roman de Roncevaux*, or perhaps, for *O*, *Bataille de Roncevaux*. rev: Roques, *Romania*, LXXX (1959), 110; De Cesare, *SF*, III (1959), 461; Menéndez Pidal, *CCM*, III (1960), 359.

In modern scholarly usage, it commonly refers to the Oxford version (*O*), in assonance, the oldest French MS. extant. But it is also employed to designate all the medieval poetic versions in French, namely, in addition to *O*, the text in assonance found in MS. Venice 4 (*V4*), the rhymed MSS Venice 7 (*V7*), Paris (*P*), Châteauroux (*C*), Cambridge (*T*), Lyon (*L*), and the short fragments in the dialect of Lorraine called *fragments Michelant* and *fragments Lavergne*. One now adds the *fragment Bogdanow* (57).

EDITIONS

The only attempt to present the whole medieval *R* tradition is:

38　Mortier, Raoul, ed. *Les Textes de la CR*. 10 vols. Paris: Editions de la Geste Francor, 1940-4.

> Published clandestinely. Vol. I: *O*; II: *V4*; III: the *Pseudo-Turpin Chronicle* in Latin and Old French, a tr. of the Provençal *Ronsasvals* by Robert Barroux, and the *Carmen de prodicione Guenonis*; IV: *C*; V: *V7* in photographic reproduction; VI: *P*; VII: *T;* VIII: *L*; IX: the *fragments Michelant* and the *fragments Lavergne*; X: Conrad's *Ruolantes Liet* in photographic reproduction and tr. by Jean Graff. Projected, but never published, were vols to contain Branch VIII of the *Karlamagnús saga*, Stricker's *Karl der Grosse*, *Karl Meinet*, the versions in Welsh, English, and Dutch, and a table of proper names and toponyms. Extremely useful for comparative purposes, since it enables one to find corresponding passages in the various versions which, when practical, are numbered according to *O*.

Whether the French texts and some of the foreign versions can be used to reconstruct an original is a matter of considerable controversy. A critical edition was first attempted by:

39 Stengel, Edmund, ed. *Das altfranzösische Rolandslied: Kritische Ausgabe.* Vol. I: Text, Variantenapparat und vollständiges Narnenverzeichnis. Leipzig: Dieterichsche Verlagsbuchhandlung: 1900.

Vol. II was never published. Based on a stemma consisting of several families (as opposed to Müller's, 44, which has only two). *O* is, in general, to be corrected when *V4* agrees with any other family against it.

The modern representative of this line of reasoning is:

40 Segre, Cesare, ed. *La Chanson de Roland: Edizione critica.* (Documenti di Filologia, XVI) Milan and Naples: Ricciardi, 1971.

Excellent introduction on the problems of editing the *CR*. Opposes both Bédier's excessive reliance on *O* and Menéndez Pidal's concept of a tradition deriving from oral transmission. Extensive critical apparatus, including whole episodes not represented in *O*. List of previous editions and good bibliography. rev: Brault, *CCM*, XVI (1973), 345-7; Delbouille, *RPh,* XXVIII (1974-5), 325-42.

The great majority of editions are based solely or principally on *O,* whose *editio princeps* was:

41 Michel, Francisque, ed. *La Chanson de Roland ou de Roncevaux du XIIᵉ siècle, publiée pour la première fois d'après le manuscrit de la Bibliothèque Bodléienne à Oxford.* Paris: Silvestre, 1837.

Both a transcription and a photographic edition of *O* have been published:

42 Stengel, Edmund, ed. *Das altfranzösische Rolandslied: Genauer Abdruck der Oxforder Handschrift Digby 23.* Heilbronn: Henninger, 1878.

43 Samaran, Charles, ed. *La Chanson de Roland: Reproduction phototypique du ms. Digby 23 de la Bodleian Library d'Oxford.* Preface by Count Alexandre de Laborde. Historical and Paleographic Study by Charles Samaran. (SATF, LXXVII) Paris: SATF, 1933. First printed for the Roxburghe Club, London, 1932.

Among the editions published before 1955, a number are still useful either for purposes of textual criticism or on account of the authority of their editors.

44 Müller, Theodor, ed. *La Chanson de Roland: Nach der Oxforder Handschrift von neuen herausgegeben, erläutert, und mit einem Glossar versehen.* Third ed., Göttingen: Dieterichsche Buchhandlung, 1878.

Established the classification followed by most editors, and to the extreme by Bédier. Two families of MSS: *O* on the one hand, and on the other all remaining texts. Only if all other versions differ from *O* can one contemplate correcting it, and even then the editor may exercise his discretion.

45 Bédier, Joseph, ed. and tr. *La Chanson de Roland, publiée d'après le manuscrit d'Oxford et traduite.* Ed. définitive. Paris: Piazza [1937].

Originally published in 1921. Repr. many times as the most popular ed. of the *CR*. Adheres to the reading of *O* in all cases except where a scribal error is obvious.

46 Lerch, Eugen, ed. *Das altfranzösische Rolandslied: Abdruck der Oxforder Handschrift in lesbarer Gestalt nebst den wichtigsten Besserungsvorschlägen der bisherigen Herausgeber.* Second, revised ed. Baden-Baden: Verlag für Kunst und Wissenschaft, 1952.

First published Munich: Hueber, 1923. Handy for comparing readings.

47 Jenkins, T. Atkinson, ed. *La Chanson de Roland: Oxford Version.* Edition, Notes, and Glossary. (Heath's Modern Language Series) Boston: D.C. Heath and Co., 1924. Revised ed.: 1929. Repr. 1954.

The text of *O* is given in reconstructed Francien dialect. The notes are still quite valuable, however, as is the Introduction, provided one is acquainted with the later critical literature. The Glossary gives etymologies.

48 Hilka, Alfons, ed. *Das altfranzösische Rolandslied nach der Oxforder Handschrift.* Fifth ed. revised by Gerhard Rohlfs. (SRÜ, III-IV) Tübingen: Niemeyer, 1960. Sixth ed.: 1965.

Originally published in 1926, this edition has been updated periodically in the light of the latest research. The resulting text is emended considerably from *O*, and is much less conservative than Bédier's.

49 Bertoni, Giulio, ed. *La Chanson de Roland.* Introduzione, testo, versione, note, glossario. Editio maior. Florence: Olschki, 1936.

Based on *O*, but with extensive emendations from *V4*.

50 Roncaglia, Aurelio, ed. *La Chanson de Roland*. (Istituto di Filologia Romanza della Univ. di Roma, Collezione di Testi e Manuali, XXVII) Modena: Società Tipografica Modenese, 1947.

The Appendix contains relevant texts of the *Annales Laurissenses*, the Annals of Pseudo-Einhard, the *Vita Karoli*, the *Vita Hludovici Imperatoris*, and Einhard the Steward's Epitaph. The first edition, 1940, presented only selections.

51 Whitehead, Frederick, ed. *La Chanson de Roland*. (Blackwell's French Texts) Oxford: Blackwell, 1970.

Repr. of the second edition, 1946. First published in 1942.

Only two entirely new editions of *O* have been published since the Second World War:

52 Calin, William, ed. *La Chanson de Roland*. (Series in Medieval French Literature) New York: Appleton-Century-Crofts, 1968.

A student edition. Footnotes translate difficult words. rev: Jones, *MLJ*, LIII (1969), 216-17; Whitehead, *FS*, XXIV (1970), 164-5; Hendrickson, *FrR*, XLV (1971-2), 298-9.

53 Moignet, Gérard, ed. and tr. *La Chanson de Roland*. Texte original établi d'après le ms. d'Oxford, traduction, notes et commentaires. (Bibliothèque Bordas, I) Paris: Bordas, 1969. Also New York: Larousse, 1969.

Useful commentary, with notes from previous scholarship. rev: Gardette, *RLiR*, XXXIII (1969), 131-2, 417; Merk, *Bulletin de la Fac. des Lettres de l'Univ. de Strasbourg*, XLVIII (1969-70), 415-17; Di Stefano, *SF*, XIV (1970), 123; Wathelet-Willem, *MR*, XX (1970), 143-4; Burgess, *MLR*, LXVI (1971), 685-6; Faigan, *AUMLA*, XXXV (1971), 127; Short, *RPh*, XXV (1971-2), 131-5; Whitehead, *FS*, XXVI (1972), 182; Drzewicka, *Kwartalnik Neofilologiczny*, XX (1973), 231-4. See also Gérard Moignet, "Correction à une édition de la *CR*." *IL*, XXIII (1971), 228-9.

Venice 4, a fourteenth-century MS. in assonance, has received considerable attention since it contains many readings which are more satisfactory than those of *O*. The standard edition, to be used in preference to Mortier's, is:

54 Gasca Queirazza, Giuliano, S. J., ed. and tr. *La CR nel testo assonanzato franco-italiano*. (L'Orifiamma, Collezione di Testi Romanzi o Mediolatini, I) Turin: Rosenberg e Sellier, 1954.

Facing-page Italian tr., Glossary, Table of Correspondences with the eds. of Kölbing and Mortier, from whose numbering G.G.Q. differs. See Geoffrey Mellor, "Some Comments on the Text of the Franco-Italian *R*." *MLR*, LXI (1966), 401-8.

The rhymed versions have been edited apart by:

55   Foerster, Wendelin, ed. *Das altfranzösische Rolandslied:*
      Text von Châteauroux und Venedig VII. (Altfranzösische
      Bibliothek, VI) Heilbronn: Henninger, 1883. Repr.
      Amsterdam: Rodopi, 1967.
      C with variants from *V7.*

56   —, ed. *Das altfranzösische Rolandslied: Text von Paris,*
      Cambridge, Lyon, und den sogennanten lothringischen
      Fragmenten. Mit Robert Heiligbrodt's Concordanztabelle
      zum altfranzösischen Rolandslied. (Altfranzösische
      Bibliothek, VII) Heilbronn: Henninger, 1886. Repr.
      Wiesbaden: Sändig, 1968.

A new fragment, closer to *T* than to the other texts of the rhyming
tradition, has come to light:

57   Bogdanow, Fanni, ed. "Un Fragment méconnu de la *CR*
      (version rimée). (Musée Britannique, Add. 41295.G.)"
      Romania, LXXXI (1960), 500-20.
      160 lines from the Episode of Baligant, with *vers orphelin*, dating from
      the end of the thirteenth c. and written in a common literary language
      with a few Western and Northeastern dialect traits. Photographs. rev:
      De Cesare, *SF*, V (1961), 514-15.

TEXTUAL CRITICISM AND DESCRIPTION OF MANUSCRIPTS

Bédier maintained that the version found in *O* was *précellent* over all
others (28). As his ideas have come to exercise less influence on *R*
scholarship, the other MSS have gradually been accorded the attention
which they deserve. The main problem has been to distinguish textual
phenomena which bespeak a history of oral transmission from those
which are due to scribal practices. Ramón Menéndez Pidal has been
the principal spokesman for those who believe that the MS. readings
reveal an oral tradition at work; Cesare Segre has pursued a more
traditional course with written transmission in view. Other scholars
have helped to clarify the relations between *R* MSS, and, ultimately,
the mode of existence of the poetic *R* tradition.

57A   Burger, André. "La Lacune du ms. *O* de la *CR* et la fin de la
      deuxième bataille." *Studia Neophilologica*, XXVII (1955),
      3-12.
      A double folio was missing in the copy from which the alpha family is
      descended.

58   Menéndez Pidal, Ramón. "Margariz de Sibilie en la tradición rolandiana." *FR*, III (1956), 1-10.
The textual tradition of the Episode of Margariz (vv. 1311-19 in *O*) shows that a binary classification (Müller-Bédier) is unreliable.

59   Rosellini, Aldo. "Un caso curioso nella *CR*: Margariz de Sibilie." *ZRP*, LXXIV (1958), 245-51. rev: De Cesare, *SF*, III (1959), 461.
Proposes a MS. division based on this episode: *V4, L, n* (the Norse version), *O, C-V7, P-T.*

60   Rosier, Jeanne. "L'Evolution du *R*." Thesis: Paris, 1958.

61   Rosellini, Aldo. "Etude comparative des mss. de Châteauroux et de Venise VII de la *CR*." *MA*, LXVI (1960), 259-300.
C and *V7* are not as closely related as some have supposed.

62   Segre, Cesare. "Tradizione fluttante della *CR* ? " *SM*, I (1960), 72-98.
Müller and Bédier preferred over Menéndez Pidal. rev: De Cesare, *SF*, V (1961), 316.

63   ——. "Un progetto di edizione critica della *CR*, e la posizione stemmatica di *n* e di *V4*." *CN*, XXI (1961), 20-33.
The crucial importance of the Norse version and *V4* in C.S.'s stemma (40).

64   Whitehead, Frederick. "The Textual Criticism of the *CR*. An Historical Review." *Ewert Studies*, pp. 76-89.
Examines the principles of Stengel, Luquiens, Bédier, and Vinaver, advocating a combination of Bédier's ideas with the traditional concept of the textual critic as a weigher of probabilities. rev: Gallais, *CCM*, VIII (1965), 440-1.

65   Thomov, Thomas S. "Le ms. *V4* dans ses rapports avec la version oxonienne de la *CR*." *Godishnik na Sofijskija Universitet, Filosofsko-istoricheski Fakultet*, LVIII, no. 1 (1964), 225-84. Also in *XI Congreso*, vol. II, pp. 777-96.
O is demonstrably superior to *V4* and the rhymed versions. rev: Gougenheim, *Romania*, LXXXVII (1966), 425-6; Dembowski, *RPh*, XXI (1967-8), 566-7.

66   Ruggieri, Ruggero M. "Alda la Bella a Vienna e a Blaia. Dati e resultati di un raddronto tra il primo *R rimé* e i *Fatti di Spagna*." *BRABLB*, XXXI (1965-6), 265-72.
The Episode of Alda as found in the *Fatti di Spagna* derives neither from *V4* nor from *C*, but rather from their common archetype, through oral transmission.

67   Segre, Cesare. "Il problema delle lasse assonanzate nei codici rimati della *CR*." *BRABLB*, XXXI (1965-6), 295-311.
Blocks of laisses in assonance were inserted into the rhymed versions, a phenomenon viewed as incompatible with the theory of oral transmission.

68   —. "La Première 'Scène du cor' dans la *CR* et la méthode de travail des copistes." *Mélanges Lejeune*, vol. II, pp. 871-89.
The scribes actively attempted to improve the text.

69   Teague, A. G. "A Re-examination of the Position of the Oxford MS. of the *CR* in Relation to the Other Versions, with Special Reference to the Evidence Offered by Konrad's *Rolandslied*." Thesis: Oxford, 1969-70.

69A   Arinaga, Hiroto. *"Roran no uta* no chūshaku to sono mondaiten, I [Commentary on the *CR* and disputed points in the original text, I]." *Tōhoku Daigaku Bungakubu Kenkyū Nenpō*, XX (1970), 165-265.

69B   ... *"Roran no uta* no chūshaku to sono mondaiten, II." *Tōhoku Daigaku Bungakubu Kenkyū Nenpō*, XXI (1972), 57-122.
These two articles constitute a line-by-line commentary on textual and philological problems, with reference to the author's 1965 tr. of the *CR* (168).

70   Burger, André. "Sur la place respective de *V4* et de *n* dans la tradition des textes rolandiens." *TLL*, VIII (1970), 277-85.
Considers the Müller-Bédier theory more accurate than that devised by Segre according to which the Norse version rather than *V4* is the best representative of its family.

71   Heinemann, Edward A. "The *Roman de Roncevaux*: Prolegomena to a Study of the MS. Tradition of the *CR*." Thesis: Princeton, 1970. *DAI*, XXXI (1970), 2878-A.

72   —. "Sur la valeur des manuscrits rimés pour l'étude de la tradition rolandienne: Tentative pour trouver les filiations des mss. *TLP*." *MA*, LXXX (1974), 71-87.
Proposes a stemma for the rhymed versions on the basis of a passage corresponding to laisses 91-106 of *O*.

73   Schlyter, Kerstin. *Les Enumérations des personnages dans la CR: Etude comparative.* (Etudes Romanes de Lund, XXII) Lund: Gleerup, 1974.

The forms of proper names are studied as a particular kind of textual variant, with the conclusion that it is impossible to draw up a coherent stemma of MS. filiation for the *R* tradition. An elegant corroboration of Menéndez Pidal's theory that the MS. tradition can only be explained as resulting from oral transmission (541-2).

74   —. "Les Enumérations de personnages dans la *CR*." *Congrès d'Aix*, pp. 159-74.

Summary of the preceding.

75   Zarri, Gian Piero. "Premiers essais de solution algorythmique des problèmes de contamination dans la *CR*." *Congrès d'Aix*, pp. 109-46.

An attempt to quantify the relations between possible combinations of three MSS on the basis of Dom Quentin's principles in order to determine which of the three is "intermediary". The author collaborated with Cesare Segre. Interpretation of the results is withheld pending further work.

O has received particular attention from textual and linguistic critics:

76   Legge, M. Dominica. "Archaism and the Conquest." *MLR*, LI (1956), 227-9.

O may have belonged to the Constable of Oxford's family, the d'Oillis. Since the survival of medieval MSS depends to a large extent on chance, it is difficult to conclude that English literary taste was old-fashioned in the twelfth c. on the basis of what is extant.

77   Noyer-Weidner, Alfred. "Eine problematische Stelle im Oxforder *R*: Karls Rückkehr aus Spanien (*O* 3682-3704)." *Festschrift Rheinfelder*, pp. 238-57.

The passage is an interpolation intended to publicize the shrine at Saint-Romain. rev: Müller, *ZFSL*, LXXV (1965), 83-5.

78   Aebischer, Paul. "Sur le vers 1776 du *R* d'Oxford." *Mélanges Lombard*, pp. 17-21.

Fors s'en eissirent li Sarrazin dedenz. The curious juxtaposition of *fors* and *dedenz* calls for emending the latter word to *espans*.

79   Lecoy, Félix. "Notules sur le texte du *R* d'Oxford." *Mélanges Lejeune*, vol. II, pp. 793-800.

Suggestions occasioned by a perusal of the photographic copy of *O*: vv. 72, 1353, 1926, 2004, 2445, 2476, 2767, 2843, 3049, 3371, 3758.

80   Thomov, Thomas S. "Sur la langue de la version oxonienne de la *CR*." *Heidelberg Colloquium*, pp. 179-93.

The Anglo-Normanisms can be imputed to the scribe and do not necessarily indicate that the author wrote in that dialect.

81   Segre, Cesare. "Corrections mentales pour la *CR*." *TLL*, VIII (1970), 277-85.
Vv. 855-6, 1631, 2060-5, 2262-3, 2633-5.

82   ——. "Errori di assonanza e rimaneggiamenti di copertura nel codice *O* della *CR*." *Un augurio a Raffaele Mattioli.* Florence: Sansoni, 1970. Pp. 465-77.
Some errors in assonance are found typically at the beginnings of laisses. The scribe adjusted or changed assonating words in the same laisses (*rimaneggiamenti di copertura*) to cover his mistakes. rev: Lecoy, *Romania*, XCIII (1972), 143-4.

83   Short, Ian. "R's Final Combat." *CN*, XXX (1970), 135-55.
A jongleur, *remanieur*, or scribe altered the form of laisses 169-70 (vv. 2271-96). *Tirer(es)* in v. 2283 refers to the pulling of R's beard, found in all MSS except *O*, an act which was originally the prime element of the passage in question.

84   Whitehead, Frederick. "Comment on Three Passages from the Text of the Oxford *R*." *History and Structure of French: Essays in Honour of Thomas Bertram Wallace Reid.* Oxford: Blackwell, 1972. Pp. 257-62.
Vv. 509, 1421, 1444.

85   Heinemann, Edward A. "La Composition stylisée et la transmission écrite des textes rolandiens." *Congrès d'Aix*, pp. 253-72.
Variations in the readings of the combat between Aelroth and R (corresponding to *O*, vv. 1200-12) need not be explained by oral transmission.

85A   Segre, Cesare. *La tradizione della CR.* (Documenti di Filologia, XVI) Milan and Naples: Ricciardi, 1974.

See also below under PARTICULAR LINES AND EPISODES IN *O* in Chapter IV.

The only other MS. whose details have received considerable attention is *V4*:

86   Rosellini, Aldo. "Sul valore della traduzione della *CR* contenuta nel manoscritto franco-italiano di *V4*." *ZRP*, LXXIV (1958), 234-45.
The tr.'s French was inadequate to his task. rev: De Cesare, *SF*, III (1959), 286-7.

87   Pellegrini, Giovanni Battista. "Osservazioni sulla lingua francoveneta di *V4*." *VIII Congresso*, pp. 707-17.

The dialect traits of *V4* resemble most closely those of Padua and Treviso.

88 Rosellini, Aldo. "Di nuovo sul valore della traduzione della *CR* del manoscritto *V4*." *SF*, X (1960), 1-10.

V4 is the work of two translators.

89 ——. *Rolandiana Marciana: Il manoscritto V4 nell'insieme della tradizione testuale della CR*. (Civiltà Veneziana, Saggi, XII) Venice: Fondazione Giorgio Cini, 1962.

A detailed analysis of *V4*, which the author believes is the work of two translators and derives from a tradition anterior to that of *O*. *O* and *V4* are nearly identical in the sections in which they correspond. The archetype of *V4* was a sort of encyclopedia of Roncevaux legends. The translator-revisers show familiarity with the rhymed versions. *V4* was composed to be read rather than recited. rev: Stussi, *SM*, IV (1963), 393-4; Boni, *SF*, VIII (1964), 290-2; Segre, *ZRP*, LXXX (1964), 147-54; A. Foulet, *RPh*, XVIII (1964-5), 367-9. See also 22.

90 Mandach, André de. "Evolution et structure de la laisse. Analyse de quelques chaînes de transmission orale, écrite et mixte." *BRABLB*, XXXI (1965-6), 153-65.

The preamble of *V4* proves that the version contained in it was meant to be sung, and supports the contention that it lived in oral tradition.

91 ——. "La Vie de la chancellerie épique des Gonzague de Mantoue." *BHR*, XXVI (1964), 621-33.

Observations on several papers dealing with the MS. tradition of the *CR*, given at the Second Congress of the Société Rencesvals (Venice, 1961). *V4* results from both oral and written stages of transmission.

92 Menéndez Pidal, Ramón. "Sobre las variantes del códice rolandiano *V4* de Venecia." *CN*, XXI (1961), 10-19.

Many of *V4*'s readings are archaic because of the MS's position on the periphery of French culture. R.M.P. distinguishes between his ideas on oral transmission of the epic through memorisation, and the Parry-Lord theory of oral composition through improvisation.

See also 28, 35, 121, 529, 530, 533, 540, 541, 542.

DATING

The problem of origins is also one of dating; thus works on the dating of the earliest traces of a *CR* are included below under the heading of ORIGINS, GENESIS, AND SOURCES in Chapter V. Studies dealing with the date of *O* or its archetype are:

93 Roncaglia, Aurelio. "Il silenzio del *R* su Sant' Iacopo: Le vie dei pellegrinaggi e le vie della storia." *Coloquios de*

Roncesvalles, pp. 151-71.
The absence of any mention of Santiago de Compostela in *O* may be explained by a break between the Papacy and the Bishop of Santiago in the period 1049-95.

94 Richthofen, Erich von. "Style and Chronology in the Early Romance Epic." *Bollettino del Centro di Studi Filologici e Linguistici Siciliani*, VIII (1962: *Saggi e ricerche in memoria di Ettore Li Gotti*, III), 83-96. Spanish tr. in *Nuevos estudios*, pp. 110-28.
Attempts to fix the date of *O* between 1095 and 1098 by combining the chronology of certain stylistic features with the hypothesis that Turoldus of Peterborough was the author.

95 Duitte, C. "Sur la date de la *CR*: Etude des problèmes relatifs à la datation de la version conservée par le ms. Digby 23 de la Bodleian Library d'Oxford." Thesis: Liège, 1964.

96 Pellegrini, Silvio. "La data della *Canzone di Rolando*." *Studi rolandiani*, pp. 75-121.
The *CR* was first composed around the middle of the eleventh c., perhaps in the second quarter, and was based on learned sources.

97 Marichal, Robert. "Paléographie latine et française." *Annuaire de l'Ecole Pratique des Hautes Etudes, IVe Section*, 1969-70. Pp. 363-74.
Report on a course which examined MS. Digby 23. *O* is dated, on the basis of the hand, closer to 1125 than to 1150. Observations on AOI, correcting Bédier's description of its distribution, and on the abbreviation 7.

98 Short, Ian. "The Oxford MS. of the *CR*: A Paleographic Note." *Romania*, XCIV (1973), 221-31.
The ligature of the *de* group is evidence for a dating in the period 1150-70.

99 Samaran, Charles. "Sur la date approximative du *R* d'Oxford." *Romania*, XCIV (1973), 523-7.
In answer to Ian Short, C.S. reaffirms his original dating of *O* (43) in the second quarter of the twelfth c.

See also 28, 29, 36, 43, 283, 486, 487, 488, 541, 542, 579, 585, 586, 593, 594, 609.

MEDIEVAL VERSIONS IN LANGUAGES OTHER THAN FRENCH

Scandinavian versions. During the course of his reign (1217-63), King Hákon Hákonarson of Norway had a number of French legends translated into Old Norse, among which were a series of episodes concerning Charlemagne known collectively as the *Karlamagnús saga*. Two of the eight sections are of prime interest for *R* studies: the First Branch is a collection of tales, mostly based on *chansons de geste*, concerning the events leading up to Roncevaux; the Eighth Branch is the translation of a *Chanson de Roland*. The Old French texts represented in translation are from a previous age, some from as far back as the eleventh c., and are thus the most direct source of information about *chansons de geste* now either lost or extant only in more recent forms. Later compilations in Swedish and Danish are based upon the *Karlamagnús saga*. The Scandinavian tradition is described in:

100   Aebischer, Paul. "Les Différents Etats de la *Karlamagnús saga*." *Fragen und Forschungen im Bereich und Umkreis der germanischen Philologie. Festgabe für Theodor Frings zum 70. Geburtstag.* (Veröffentlichungen des Instituts für Deutsche Sprache und Literatur der Deutschen Akademie der Wissenschaften zu Berlin, VIII) Berlin: Akademie-Verlag, 1956. Pp. 298-322.
Relations between the various versions, including the Danish *Karl Magnus Krønike*.

101   ——. "*Karlamagnús saga, Keiser Karl Krønike* danoise et *Karl Magnus* suédois." *SN*, XXIX (1957), 145-79. Repr. in *Rolandiana et Oliveriana*, pp. 273-302.
Four successive states of the *Karlamagnús saga* are discernible, all compiled in the course of the thirteenth c. rev: Favati, *SF*, III (1959), 116.

101A   Togeby, Knud. "L'Influence de la littérature française sur les littératures scandinaves au moyen âge." *Grundriss der romanischen Literaturen des Mittelalters.* Edited by Hans Robert Jauss and Erich Köhler. Vol. I: *Généralités.* Heidelberg: Carl Winter, Universitätsverlag, 1972. Pp. 333-95.
Karlamagnús saga: pp. 354-67; see also pp. 376-7, 386, 388-91, 393. The *Karlamagnús saga* was compiled by a French *remanieur*. Branch VIII is descended from *O*.

The standard ed. of the Old Norse text is Unger's (1860); a modernized version is:

102   Vilhjálmsson, Bjarni, ed. *Karlamagnús saga og kappa hans.* 3 vols. Reykjavik: Islendingasagnaútgáfan, Haukadalsútgáfan, 1954.
Spelling is normalized. Introduction and Index of Proper Names.

The First Branch has been translated and studied by:

103   Aebischer, Paul. *Textes norrois et littérature française du*

moyen âge. Vol. I. *Recherches sur les traditions épiques antérieures à la CR d'après les données de la première branche de la Karlamagnús saga.* (PRF, XLIV), Geneva: Droz, 1954.

A French compilation, which P.A. calls the *Vie romancée de Charlemagne*, would be the source of the First Branch, which is the earliest part of the saga and inspired the translation of other epic materials.

104 ——. *Textes norrois et littérature française du moyen âge.* Vol. II. *La première branche de la Karlamagnús saga.* Traduction complète du texte norrois, précédée d'une introduction et suivie d'un index des noms propres cités. (PRF, CXVIII) Geneva: Droz, 1972.

A literal tr. of the First Branch, in which Ganelon's hatred arises from an incident in which R. makes love to Ganelon's second wife, Geluviz. Other matters of direct relevance for *R* criticism in this fascinating text are the account of R's birth (the *péché de Charlemagne*), R's childhood exploits, the taking of Nobles (*O*, vv. 198, 1775), the origin of Durendal and the relics in its hilt, and a medieval etymology of the war-cry *Monjoie*. rev: Williams, *FrR*, XLVI (1972-3), 1003-4; Gilbert and Van Emden, *CCM*, XVI (1973), 149-54; Ross, *MAe*, XLIII (1974), 159; Horrent, *MA*, LXXX (1974), 358-9.

See also 503, 503A, 536, 545, 568.

The Eighth Branch has been studied by:

105 Aebischer, Paul. *Rolandiana Borealia: La Saga af Runzivals Bardaga et ses dérivés scandinaves comparés à la CR.* Essai de restauration du ms. français utilisé par le traducteur norrois. (Univ. de Lausanne. Publ. de la Fac. des Lettres, XI) Lausanne: Rouge et Compagnie, Librairie de l'Univ., 1954.

Includes a complete tr. Gives an account of the Scandinavian versions, a critique of the translator, and a detailed running commentary comparing the saga with *O*, and at times other MSS. *O* would be lacking an ending, one which is found in the Danish *Karl Magnus Krønike*. The text of which the Eighth Branch is a tr. belongs to the *beta* family of *R* MSS rather than to the same family as *O*, and is the earliest MS. in that family of whose content we have evidence. It was written in the Anglo-Norman dialect and dates from the second half of the twelfth c., possibly from the first half. *O* is the product of a *remanieur de génie*. The Eighth Branch does not contain an Episode of Baligant. P.A.'s book is a major contribution. rev: Lecoy, *Romania*, LXXVI (1955), 386; Lausberg, *Archiv*, CXCIII (1956), 227; Frings, *ZRP*, LXXIII (1957), 182.

106   Halvorsen, E. F. *The Norse Version of the CR.* (Bibliotheca Arnamagnaeana, XIX) Copenhagen: Munksgaard, 1959.

Studying the differences between the Eighth Branch and the hypothetical contents of the Anglo-Norman MS. (*k*) of which it is a more or less faithful tr., E.F.H. is more willing than Aebischer to ascribe some anomalies to variations which would already have been present in *k*, notably for the Episode of Baligant, which he believes to have been absent from *k*. The latter would have been composed around 1150, perhaps even before, and was shorter than any other surviving version. Its author was probably a Norwegian cleric who had studied in England. rev: Nykrog, *Studia Neophilologica*, XXXII (1960), 376-9.

106A   Clover, Carol. "Scene in Saga Composition." *Arkiv för Nordisk Filologi*, LXXXIX (1974), 57-83.

The Norse translator did not merely translate or adapt: he recomposed the tale into tripartite scenes.

See also 63, 70.

The Swedish derivative has been edited and studied by:

107   Kornhall, David, ed. *Karl Magnus enligt Codex Verelianus och Fru Elins bok.* (Samlingar, Utgivna av Svenska Fornskriftsällskapet, Häft 219, Bd. LXIII) Lund: Blomsboktryckeri, 1957.

108   ——. *Den fornsvenska sagan om Karl Magnus: Handskrifter och texthistoria.* With a Summary in English. (Lundastudier i Nordisk Språkvetenskap, XV) Lund: Gleerup, 1959.

The MSS, origin, and development of *Karl Magnus.*

For the Danish derivative, see:

109   Hjort, Poul Lindegård. *Karl Magnus' Krønike.* (Universitetsjubilaeets Danske Samfund Skriftserie, CCCXCVIII) Copenhagen: Schulz, 1960.

109A   ——. "Filologiske studier over *Karl Magnus' Krønike.*" Unpubl. thesis: Copenhagen, 1964.

The Pseudo-Turpin Chronicle. Over 300 Latin and vernacular MSS of this work, originally composed around 1140, have survived from the Middle Ages. Purporting to come from the pen of Turpin, it was probably compiled as the fourth section of the five-part *Liber Sancti Jacobi* of Pseudo-Calixtus II, a guide for pilgrims making their way to Santiago de Compostela. Since the *Pseudo-Turpin Chronicle* will be the subject of another bibliography in this series, only the most important publications are given here. At present, the most comprehensive bibliography of *Pseudo-Turpin* studies will be found in 550, vol. I.

110   Meredith-Jones, Cyril, ed. *Historia Karoli Magni et Rotholandi, ou, Chronique du Pseudo-Turpin.* Textes revus et publiés d'après 49 mss. Paris: Droz, 1936.
The Introduction includes discussion of the work's origins.

111   Walpole, Ronald N. "Sur la *Chronique du Pseudo-Turpin.*" *TLL*, vol. III (1965), no. 2, pp. 7-18.
An introduction to the *Pseudo-Turpin* which concludes that its author may have been a monk at Saint-Denis.

112   Mandach, André de. "L'Ouvrage de Turpin est-il vraiment une chronique en prose? Une comparaison entre l'art poétique de Turpin et de Turoldus (résumé)." *CCM*, III (1960), 71-5.
The scene of the *Pseudo-Turpin* in which R bids adieu to Durendal is poetry rather than prose

113   Short, Ian, ed. *The Anglo-Norman Pseudo-Turpin Chronicle of William de Briane.* (Anglo-Norman Text Society, XXV) Oxford: Blackwell, 1973.
Ed. of the third in date (second decade of the thirteenth c.) among French translations of the *Pseudo-Turpin*, prefaced by a study of the translator and his patrons, the sources, the tr. itself, the MS., and the language. Glossary. rev: *TLS*, March 29, 1974, p. 321.

114   Hämel, Adalbert, and André de Mandach, eds. *Der Pseudo-Turpin von Compostela.* (Bayerische Akademie der Wissenschaften, Philosophisch-historische Klasse, Sitzungsbericht, 1965. Vol. I) Munich: Beck, 1965.
rev: Aebischer, *CCM*, IX (1966), 261; Ziltener, *ZRP*, LXXXIII (1967), 119-24; Guiter, *RLR*, LXXVIII (1968), 209; Minis, *Neophilologus*, LII (1968), 89-90.

See also 38, 133, 138, 141A, 224, 550, 557, 599, 609, 614, 623.

The Ruolantes Liet. The dating of this clerical adaptation of the *CR* by the priest Conrad depends on the identification of a Duke Henry and his wife who are mentioned in the epilogue. Current opinion, subsequent to the work of Dieter Kartschoke, seems to favor a period around 1170. In the first half of the thirteenth c., a man known as *der Stricker* reworked the *Ruolantes Liet* in a rhymed version known as *Karl der Grosse.* Only the most important studies and those directly relevant to the *CR* are given here, since Conrad's work has become an object of considerable scholarly activity among Germanists.

115   Wesle, Carl, ed. *Das Rolandslieds des Pfaffen Konrad.* Second ed. (Altdeutsche Texte für den Akademischen Unterricht, III) Halle: Max Niemeyer Verlag, 1963.

116   —. *Das Rolandslied des Pfaffen Konrad.* Second ed. with an Introduction by Peter Wapnewski. (Altdeutsche Textbibliothek, LXIX) Tübingen: Max Niemeyer Verlag, 1967.
       Extensive bibliography, pp. xxi-xxxi. The Introduction treats the *Ruolantes Liet* as a literary artifact and reviews research devoted to it. rev: Di Stefano, *SF*, XII (1968), 519.

117   Kartschoke, Dieter, ed. and tr. *Das Rolandslied des Pfaffen Konrad.* Mittelhochdeutscher Text mit Übertragung. (Bücher des Wissens) Frankfurt am Main: Fischer Bücherei, 1970.
       The afterword includes a short bibliography.

118   Wisbey, Roy A. *A Complete Concordance to the Rolandslied (Heidelberg MS.).* With Word Indexes to the Fragmentary MSS by Clifton Hall. Leeds: Maney, 1969.
       Includes a Reverse Index, an Index of Rhymes, a Frequency List, and a Finding List of Verb Forms. rev: Ross, *MLR*, LXVI (1971), 209-10.

119   Kartschoke, Dieter. *Die Datierung des Deutschen Rolandsliedes.* (Germanistische Abhandlungen, IX) Stuttgart: Metzler, 1965.
       rev: Ashcroft, *FMLS*, V (1969), 262-80.

119A   Richter, Horst. *Kommentar zum Rolandslied des Pfaffen Konrad.* (Kanadische Studien zur Deutschen Sprache und Literatur, VI) Berne, Frankfurt: Herbert Lang, 1972.
       A line-by-line commentary on the first third of Conrad's work.

The following studies treat the much-debated question of the *Ruolantes Liet's* relationship to the *CR*:

120   Mager, Elisabeth. "Das Ethos des mittelhochdeutschen *Rolandsliedes,* vergleichen mit dem der *CR.*" Thesis: Humboldt-Univ., 1962.
       Résumé in *Wissenschaftliche Zeitschrift der Humboldt-Univ. in Berlin,* Gesellschafts- und Sprachwissenschaftliche Reihe, XIII (1964), pp. 406-7.

121   Keller, Hans Erich. "La Place du *Ruolantes Liet* dans la tradition rolandienne." *MA*, LXXI (1965), 215-46, 401-21.
The French model of the *Ruolantes Liet* is the only text which follows the sequence of events as found in *O*. Contrary to Bédier's claim, all the versions other than *O* do not descend from a single reworking. The *R* tradition was in continual transformation and the *chanson de geste* as a genre was, as Menéndez Pidal maintained, "l'œuvre de tous."

122   Mager, Elisabeth. "Der Standescharakter der Tapferkeit: Ein Vergleich zwischen *CR* und mittelhochdeutschen *Rolandslied*." *Wissentschaftliche Zeitschrift der Ernst-Moritz-Arndt-Univ. Greifswald*, Gesellschafts- und Sprachwissenschaftliche Reihe, XV (1966), pp. 545-9.
Both the *CR* and the *Ruolantes Liet* are inspired by the knightly class, but the latter focusses on boldness and daring. Analysis of the concepts of *barnage, vasselage, proece, vaillance*.

123   Missfeldt, Antje. "Ein Vergleich der Laisseneinheiten in der *CR* (Hs. *O*) mit der Abschnittstechnik in Konrads *Rolandslied*." *Zeitschrift für Deutsche Philologie*, XCII (1973), 321-38.
The structure of Conrad's episode follows *O*'s laisse divisions, with some exceptions.

See also 38, 69, 330, 331, 405, 537, 599.

The Carmen de prodicione Guenonis.   The *Carmen* is a 482-line version without the Episode of Baligant; only a few lines are devoted to Ganelon's punishment.

124   Curtius, Ernst Robert. "Das *Carmen de prodicione Guenonis*." *Gesammelte Aufsätze*, pp. 81-98. Repr. from *ZRP*, LXII (1942), 492-509.
The author of the *Carmen*, a thirteenth-c. work, knew a Latin *Bellum de Runcevalle* as well as the *Pseudo-Turpin Chronicle* and the *CR*. The *Carmen* is not valid evidence for the existence of an earlier version of the *CR* without the Episode of Baligant.

124A   Schumann, Otto. "Zum *Carmen de proditione Guenonis*." *ZRP*, LXII (1942), 510-27.
Comments on the text and on reminiscences in it of other works.

See also 38.

The Dutch version. Fragments totalling 1835 lines are extant, ending before the Episode of Baligant.

125   Van Mierlo, J., S. J. *"Het Roelantslied,* met inleidung en
aanteekeningen." *Vlaamsche Academie voor Taal- en
Letterkunde. Verslagen en Letterkunde,* 1935. Ledeberg
and Gent: Erasmus, 1935. Pp. 31-166.
Ed. with critical introduction.

Roncesvalles.   A 100-line Spanish fragment of a late thirteenth-c.
Spanish epic; the MS. is fourteenth-c.

126   Horrent, Jules. *Roncesvalles: Etude sur le fragment de cantar
de gesta conservé à l'Archivo de Navarra (Pampelune).* (Bibl.
de la Fac. de Phil. et Lettres de l'Univ. de Liège, CXXII)
Paris: Société d'Edition 'Les Belles Lettres', 1951.
New ed. of the fragment (the original was by Menéndez Pidal, *RFE*, IV
[1917], 105-204), with a substantial study. Glossary and bibliography.

127   Ruggieri, Ruggero M. "Nuove osservazioni sui rapporti tra il
frammento di *Roncesvalles* e la leggenda rolandiana in
Francia e in Italia." *Coloquios de Roncesvalles,* pp. 173-88.
Various aspects treated. Concludes that the Romantic critics were, in
general, closer to the truth than their modern counterparts.

128   Riquer, Martín de. "Dos notas rolandianas. El segundo 'duc
Aymon' del fragmento de *Roncesvalles* (v. 97). Un aspecto
zaragozano del *Rollan a Saragossa* provenzal." *RFE*, XLII
(1958-9), 261-9. Revised version in *La leyenda del graal y
temas épicos medievales.* (El Soto, VI) Madrid: Prensa
Española, 1968. Pp. 200-4 and 213-20.
The second Aymon is Naimes (Naymon).   rev: Lecoy, *Romania*
LXXXIII (1962), 284-5.

128A   ——. "El fragmento de *Roncesvalles* y el planto de
Gonzalo Gústioz." *La leyenda del graal y temas épicos
medievales.* Madrid: Editorial Prensa Española, 1968. Pp.
205-13. Revised from *Studi Monteverdi,* II, 623-8.
Roncesvalles shows the influence of a version of the *Siete infantes de
Salas,* a fact which reverses the chronology posited by Menéndez Pidal.

128B   Catalán, Diego. "El *Toledano romanzado* y las *Estorias del
fecho de los Godos* del siglo XV."*Estudios dedicados a James
Homer Herriott.* Madison: Univ. of Wisconsin, 1966. Pp.
9-102.
Pp. 39-44 treat of *Roncesvalles* and the legend of Bernardo del Carpio
as they appear in the texts in question.

128C Webber, Ruth House. "The Diction of the *Roncesvalles* Fragment." *Homenaje a Rodríguez-Moñino: Estudios de erudición que le ofrecen sus amigos o discípulos hispanistas norteamericanos.* Madrid: Editorial Castalia, 1966. II, pp. 311-21.
The fragment is characterized by a formulaic style.

129 Horrent, Jacques. "L'Allusion à la chanson de *Mainet* contenue dans le *Roncesvalles.*" *MR*, XX (1970), 85-92.

See also 609, 610, 614, 623, 624.

The Provençal Ronsasvals. The fourteenth-c. fragmentary text of 1802 lines recounting the Battle of Roncevaux and events up to the death of Alda, but without mention of Baligant, was found in the register for the year 1398 of one Rostan Bonet, notary in the town of Apt, along with *Rollan a Sarragossa.* The latter tells of R's visit to Marsile's wife Braslimonde in Saragossa.

130 Roques, Mario, ed. "*Ronsasvals*, poème épique provençal." *Romania*, LVIII (1932), 1-28, 161-89.
Ed. with index of proper names.

131 Lejeune, Rita. "Une Allusion méconnue à une *CR.*" *Romania*, LXXV (1954), 151-62.
Gregori Bechada's *Canso d'Antiocha* (1130-42) alludes to the Battle of Roncevaux in terms only found in *Ronsasvals.*

132 Riquer, Martín de. "La antigüedad del *Ronsasvals* provenzal." *Coloquios de Roncesvalles*, pp. 245-51. Revised version in *La leyenda del graal* (see 128), pp. 189-99.
A twelfth-c. version of *Ronsasvals* was known to the troubadour Guilhem de Berguedán.

133 Adams, Duane Alfred. "A Re-examination of the R Legend: A Comparative Study of Selected *Matières* in the Traditions of the Oxford Version, the *Chronicle of Turpin* and the Provençal Epic Poem *Ronsasvals.*" Thesis: Louisiana State, 1963. *DA*, XXIV (1963-4), 1602.

134 Hendriks, Gerdina Johanna. "*Ronsasvals* and *Châteauroux*: Etude comparative précédée d'une analyse de la langue de *Ronsasvals.*" Thesis: Utrecht, 1967.

135 Riquer, Martín de. "La fecha del *Ronsasvals* y de *Rollan a Saragossa* según el armamento." *BRAE*, XLIX (1969), 211-51.

The texts found in the fourteenth-c. MSS differ little from versions known by troubadours in the second half of the twelfth c.

See also 38, 623.

The Middle Welsh version. Extant in at least eight MSS, this version has not been adequately studied. For an evaluation of previous scholarship, see:

136 Watkin, Morgan. "Les Traductions galloises des épopées françaises." *Gallica: Essays Presented to J. Heywood Thomas by Colleagues, Pupils, and Friends.* Cardiff: Univ. of Wales Press, 1969. Pp. 31-9.
Robert Williams' 1892 ed. of the version found in the Hengwrt MSS is unreliable.

137 Williams, Robert. "The History of Charlemagne: A Translation of *Ystorya de Carolo Magno* with a Historical and Critical Introduction." *Y Cymmrodor*, XX (1907), 1-219.
Tr. based on Thomas Powell's 1883 transcription from the *Red Book of Hergest*. The Introduction is fanciful. The text translated is close to, but not identical with, the one published in the following item. This Robert Williams is not the person who edited the Hengwrt MSS (see 136).

138 Williams, Stephen J., ed. *Ystorya de Carolo Magno, o Llyfre Coch Hergest* [The history of Ch. contained in the *Red Book of Hergest*]. Cardiff: Gwasg Prifysgol Cymru, 1968. First published 1930.
Contains the Welsh *CR*, *Pseudo-Turpin Chronicle*, and *Chanson d'Otinel.*

The Middle English version.

139 Herrtage, Sidney J., ed. *The Sege of Melayne and the Romance of Duke Rowland and Sir Otuell of Spayne. Now for the First Time Printed, with a Fragment of the Song of Roland.* (Early English Text Society, Extra Series, XXXV) London: Trübner, 1880.

The hypothetical Hungarian version.

140 Vajay, Szabolcs de. "A magyar *Roland-ének* nyomaban [On the trail of the Hungarian *CR*]." *Irodalomtörténeti Közlemények*, LXXII (1968), 333-7.
Although there is no direct trace of a medieval Hungarian version, the

occurrence of the names R and Oliver in the Ratot family argues for the existence of a thirteenth-c. text.

The Croniques et Conquestes de Charlemaine. A 1458 compilation by David Aubert.

141   Guiette, Robert. "Les Deux Scènes du cor dans la *CR* et dans les *Conquestes de Charlemagne.*" *MA*, LXIX (1963), 845-55. Repr. in *Romanica Gandensia*, XIII (1972), 91-9.

The compiler of the *Conquestes*, who depicts R as culpable and repentant, does not understand the knightly ideal, which in the *CR* renders R's act a sacred sacrifice, innocent of pride or imprudence.

141A   Schobben, J. M. G. *La Part du Pseudo-Turpin dans les "Croniques et Conquestes de Ch" de David Aubert.* (Publ. de l'Institut d'Etudes Françaises et Occitanes de l'Univ. d'Utrecht, II) The Hague: Mouton, 1969.

Chapter III treats the respective roles of the *Pseudo-Turpin Chronicle* and the *CR* in David Aubert's narration of the *R* material.

See also 554.

MODERN TRANSLATIONS AND ADAPTATIONS

With few exceptions, only translations first published after 1954, and of scholarly value, have been included.

English

142   Sayers, Dorothy L., tr. *The Song of Roland.* A New Translation. (Penguin Classics, L75) Harmondsworth: Penguin Books Ltd, 1957. Also Baltimore: Penguin Books, 1957.

rev: Whitehead, *FS*, XII (1958), 364.

143   Scott-Moncrieff, C. J., tr. *The Song of Roland.* New York: Heritage Press, 1955. Also published with an Introduction by G. K. Chesterton and a Note on Technique by George Saintsbury. (Ann Arbor Paperbacks, AA32) Ann Arbor, Michigan: Univ. of Michigan Press, 1959.

First published 1919. rev: Pei, *FrR*, XXIX (1955-6), 366; Hall, *RPh*, XIV (1960-1), 353-5.

144   Wright, Laura Moore, tr. *The Song of Roland: The Legend that Turoldus Relates.* The Oxford Version Translated into Modern English Verse. New York: Vantage Press, 1960.

145 Price, Hilda Cumings, tr. *The Song of Roland*. A New
Abridged Tr. in Verse. Illustrated by Christine Price.
London and New York: Warne, 1961.

146 Alfred, William, William S. Merwin, and Helen Mustard, tr.
Medieval Epics. (The Modern Library, G87) New York:
Random House, 1963.
Contains tr. of the *CR* (by Merwin), the *Cantar de Mio Cid*, *Beowulf*,
and the *Nibelungenlied*. rev: Jones, *Speculum*, XXXIX (1964), 191-2.

147 Merwin, William S., tr. *The Song of Roland*. New York:
Vintage Books, 1963. Repr. 1970.

148 Terry, Patricia, tr. *The Song of Roland*. Introduction and
Bibliography by Harold March. (The Library of Liberal Arts,
CCXXI) Indianapolis: Bobbs-Merrill, 1965.

149 Sherwood, Merriam, tr. *The Song of Roland*. Illustrated by
Edith Emerson. New York: McKay, 1967. First published
1938.

150 Harrison, Robert, tr. *The Song of Roland*. Translated from
the Old French with an Introduction. (Mentor Books,
MQ1023) New York: American Library, 1970.

151 Robertson, Howard S., tr. *The Song of Roland*. Translated
with an Introduction and Notes. (Everyman's Univ.
Paperbacks) London: Dent, 1972.
rev: Brault, *CCM*, XVII (1974), 77-8.

152 Owen, David Douglas Roy, tr. *The Song of Roland*. (Unwin
Classics) London: Allen and Unwin, 1972.
rev: *TLS*, August 11, 1972, p. 954; Fox, *MLR*, LXX (1975), 173.

153 ——. *The Legend of Roland: A Pageant of the Middle Ages*.
London: Phaidon, 1973.
A popularizing treatment of the legend, lavishly illustrated with medieval representations of R. The introductory chapter sketches the
current state of scholarly knowledge. A paraphrase of the poem is
followed by notes on legendary developments which follow *O*.

French

154 Cordier, André, ed. and tr. *La CR*. Extraits. Textes et
traduction d'après le ms. d'Oxford. Avec une notice bio-
graphique, une notice historique et littéraire, des notes
explicatives, des jugements, un questionnaire et des sujets de

devoirs. (Classiques Larousse) Paris: Larousse, 1958. First published 1935.

155 Thomas, Marcel, ed. and tr. *La Geste de R.* Textes épiques choisis, présentés et traduits. (Astrée, XXXIV) Paris: Club du Meilleur Livre, 1961.

156 Plazolles, Louis Robert, tr. *La CR.* Traduction originale du ms. d'Oxford et commentaires. Paris: Club du Livre, 1962.

157 Tessier, Maurice, tr. *La CR.* Traduite en français moderne d'après le ms. d'Oxford. Illustrations de Christiane Grandsaignes d'Hauterive. Paris: Lanore, 1962. First published 1947.

158 Picot, Guillaume, ed. and tr. *La CR.* Avec une notice historique et littéraire, un lexique, des notes explicatives et un questionnaire. 2 vols. (Nouveaux Classiques Larousse) Paris: Larousse, 1965.
The OFr text is given for laisses 146-85; the entire poem is translated.

159 Lhéritier, Andrée, ed. and tr. *La CR.* Edition bilingue suivie de Yves Bonnefoy, "Les mots et la parole dans le *R.*" Préface par Michel Robic. (Le Monde en 10-18, CCCXCIII-V) Paris: Union Générale d'Editions, 1968.

160 Moignet, Gérard, tr. *La CR.* Traduction d'après le ms. d'Oxford, avec une introduction, des notes, des commentaires. (Petits Classiques Bordas) Paris: Bordas, 1970.

161 Jones, George Fenwick, and Ann Demaître, tr. *La CR.* Englewood Cliffs, New Jersey: Prentice Hall, 1971.
Based on Geddes' English version (1906), which is in turn based on Müller's ed. rev: Van Emden, *FS*, XXVIII (1974), 180-1; Hendrickson, *FrR*, XLVII (1973-4), 273-4.

See also 45, 53.

German

162 Klein, Hans W., tr. and ed. *La CR.* (Klassische Texte des Romanischen Mittelalters in Zweisprachigen Ausgaben) Munich: Eidos, 1963.
rev: Kolb, *Anzeiger für Deutsches Altertum und Deutsche Literatur*, LXXIV (1963-4), 165-7.

163 Besthorn, Rudolf, and Wilhelm Hertz, tr. *Das Rolandslied.*

(Sammlung Dietrich, CCCXLI) Leipzig: Dieterichsche Verlagsbuchhandlung, 1972.
rev: Michael, *Frankfurter Allgemeine*, March 30, 1973, p. 31.

Italian

164 Raimondo, Carlo, tr. *La Canzone di Rolando nel testo di Oxford ms. Digby 23 e nella traduzione di Carlo Raimondo.* Turin: ILTE, 1956. First published 1927.
rev: Barroux, *MA*, LXIII (1957), 369-70.

165 Nardelli, Matteo, ed. and tr. *La CR*. Milan: Sigla, 1958.

166 Torrisi Cardellicchio, Concetta, tr. *La CR*. Taranto: Athena, 1964.

See also 49.

Japanese

167 Satō, Teruo, tr. *Rōran no uta* [The *CR*]. Sekai Bungaku Taikei, LXV) Tokyo: Chikuma Shobō, 1962.

168 Arinaga, Hiroto, tr. *Roran no uta* [The *CR*].
(Iwanami Bunkō) Tokyo: Iwanami Shoten, 1965.
Includes notes on the text. See 69A and 69B.

Polish

169 Drzewicka, Anna. "Jak powstał najstarszy polski przekład *Piesni o Rolandzie*" [The oldest Polish translation of the *CR*]. *Kwartalnik Neofilologiczny*, XII (1965), 145-56.

Rumanian

169A Tanase, Eugen, tr. *Cîntara lui Roland*. Bucarest: Editura Univers, 1974.
rev: Guiter, *RLR*, LXXXI (1974), 501-2.

Spanish

170 Gaya y Delrue, Marcelo, tr. *La Canción de Roldán*. Saragossa: n.p., 1959.

171 Riquer, Martín de, tr. *El Cantar de Roldán*. Traducción del texto francés del siglo XII del ms. de Oxford. Madrid:

Espasa-Calpe, 1960.
rev: Soria, *Arbor*, no. 175-6 (1960), 128-30.

172   Doddis Miranda, Antonio, tr. *Canción de Rolando.* Versión
en castellano y estudios. Selección de Antonio Doddis
Miranda y Germán Sepúlveda Durán. (Univ. de Chile.
Instituto Pedagógico. Departamento de Castellano)
Santiago: Editorial Universitaria, 1962.

173   Marquina, Eduardo, tr. *La gesta de Roldán.* Versión
castellana de la *CR*. Introducción por Ramón Castelltort.
Barcelona: Ediciones Zeus, 1962.

174   Muñiz, Enriqueta, tr. *La Canción de Rolando.* Second ed.
(Colección Clásicos Hachette) Buenos Aires: Hachette, 1962.

175   Jarnés, Benjamín, tr. *El cantar de Roldán.* Fourth ed.
(Musas Lejanas: Mitos, Cuentos, Leyendas, I) Madrid:
Revista de Occidente, 1963. First published 1926.

176   Lázaro Ros, Amando, tr. *Canción de Roldán.* (Colección
Crisol) Madrid: Aguilar, 1963.

Phonograph recordings

177   *La CR.* Folkways Records, FL 9587. 1961. Performed in
twelfth-c. French by the Proscenium Studio, Montreal.
Lucie de Vienne, Director.
Program notes and text with modern French tr. and English tr. by
Dorothy L. Sayers in album.

178   *The Song of Roland.* Caedmon, TC 2059. 1971. Tr. from
the French by Dorothy L. Sayers. Edited by Barbara
Holdridge. Read by Anthony Quayle.
Program notes by Dorothy L. Sayers on slipcase.

IV

DETAILS OF THE OXFORD VERSION

The version found in the Oxford MS. has been explicated and elucidated more than any other single work of Old French literature, not only on account of its poetic pre-eminence, but also because of its relative antiquity among OFr texts. The studies enumerated under this heading seek to clarify the meaning of words or lines, or to illuminate particular episodes. Aesthetic aspects of *O* will be dealt with in Chapter V.

SYNTAX AND MORPHOLOGY

A distinction posited by Pierre Guiraud gave rise to controversy over the meaning of inconsistencies in the case system.

179　Guiraud, Pierre. "L'Expression du virtuel dans le *R* d'Oxford." *Romania*, LXXXIII (1962), 289-302.
　　The opposition *actuel-virtuel* clarifies case usage.

180　Spence, Nicol C. W. "Existait-il en ancien français une opposition *actuel-virtuel*? " *RLiR*, XXX (1966), 353-73.
　　Disagrees with Guiraud's contention that this opposition is the key to the use of the article.

181　Guiraud, Pierre. "Le Démonstratif épique dans la *CR*." *Essais de stylistique*. Paris: Klincksieck, 1969. Pp. 191-211. Repr. from "L'assiette du nom dans la *CR*, 2: Le démonstratif." *Romania*, LXXXVIII (1967), 59-83.
　　Cil is used for space and time spoken of, *cist* for space and time lived in.

182　Woledge, Brian, J. Beard, C. H. Horton, and Ian Short. "La Déclinaison des substantifs dans la *CR*: Recherches mécanographiques." *Romania*, LXXXVIII (1967), 145-74.
　　A computer-aided study of the case system shows a more complex situation than Guiraud's distinction *actuel-virtuel* can account for. It is a matter of alternatives and tendencies rather than of rules. These conclusions are reinforced in the following item. rev: Di Stefano, *SF*, XI (1967), 513.

183　Woledge, Brian, H. M. Erk, P. B. Grout, and I. A. MacDougall.

"La Déclinaison des substantifs dans la *CR*: Recherches mécanographiques (2ème article)." *Romania*, XC (1969), 174-201.

Other studies:

184   Kishimoto, Michio. *"Rōran no uta* no dōshi goi [Verbs in the *CR*]." *Furansugo Kenkyū (ELF)*, XVII (1958), 6-11.

184A   ——. *"Rōran no uta* no dōshi goi, II [Verbs in the *CR*, II]." *Furansugo Kenkyū, (ELF)*, XVIII (1958), 42ff.

185   ——. *"Rōran no uta* no dōshi goi: Toku ni gerumango kigen no shakuyōgo ni tsuite [Verbs in the *CR*: Concerning, in particular, borrowed words of Germanic origin]." *Kobe Gaidai Ronsō*, VIII, no. 4 (1958), 125-44.

186   ——. *"Rōran no uta* no dōshi goi, III [Verbs in the *CR*, III]." *Osaka Shiritsu Daigaku Bungakkai, Jimbun Kenkyū*, XI, no. 8 (August, 1960), 15-26.

In the four articles above, the author outlines the "linguistic fields" of a number of verbs and their synonyms, tracing their philological development.

186A   ——. "Tsūjitai to kyōjitai [Diachrony and synchrony]." *Osaka Shiritsu Daigaku Bungakkai, Jimbun Kenkyū*, XI, no. 8 (August, 1960), 1-14.

Using the *CR*'s verbs as examples, the author concludes that one can only speak of synonyms in a diachronic context.

187   Moignet, Gérard. "L'Ordre verbe-sujet dans la *CR*." *Mélanges Boutière*, pp. 397-421.

Explores patterns of verb-subject inversion, some syntactical, some stylistic.

LEXICON AND SEMANTICS

An exhaustive glossary was compiled by Lucien Foulet for Bédier's *CR commentée* (28). A complete listing of forms is found in:

188   Duggan, Joseph J. *A Concordance of the CR*. Columbus: Ohio State Univ. Press, 1969.

Computer-generated. Gives the word forms in context, with line references. rev: Baldinger, *ZRP*, LXXXVI (1970), 676-7; Labarre, *BBF*, XVI (1971), 32-4; Allen, *CH*, V (1971), 245-9; Lecoy, *Romania*, XCII (1971), 575; Di Stefano, *SF*, XIV (1971), 184; Cargo, *FrR*, XLIV (1970-1), 814-15; Nichols, *Speculum*, XLVII (1972), 303-4; McMillan,

ZRP, LXXXVIII (1972), 216-21; Whitehead, *FS*, XXVI (1972), 182-4; Koenig, *RPh*, XXVI (1972-3), 204-5; Hanon, *Revue Romane*, VIII (1973), 421-3.

The origin of the French warcry "Munjoie" has continued to inspire interest:

189 Nitze, William A. "Some Remarks on the Origin of the French *Montjoie*." *RPh*, IX (1955-6), 11-17.

Against Laura Hibbard Loomis' derivation from *meum gaudium*, W.A.N. proposes the Germanic *mund gawi*, "cairn, pile of stones," which, employed as a battle cry, signifies "Hold the line!"

190 Harris, Julian. "*Munjoie* and *Reconuisance* in *CR*, Line 3620." *RPh*, X (1956-7), 168-73.

Munjoie is a cry of gratitude for God's wisdom; *reconuisance* does not mean "rallying cry." rev: Favati, *SF*, II (1958), 284.

190A Kaspers, Wilhelm. "Der Name *Montjoie* und seine Bedeutungsvarianten." *Beiträge zur Namenforschung*, IX (1958), 173-9.

Munjoie derives from Germanic *mund, "protection, protector," and *galga*, "cross."

191 Loomis, Laura Hibbard. "L'Oriflamme de France et le cri *Munjoie* au XIIe siècle." *MA*, LXV (1959), 469-99. Originally appeared as "The Oriflamme of France and the War-cry *Monjoie*." *Studies in Art and Literature for Belle da Costa Greene*. Princeton: Princeton Univ. Press, 1954. Pp. 67-82.

There is no connection between the *oriflamme* and Saint-Denis. Reaffirms the derivation of *Munjoie* from *meum gaudium*. rev: De Cesare, *SF*, IV (1960), 314.

192 Diament, Henri. "Une Interprétation hagio-toponymique de l'ancien cri de guerre des Français, *Monjoie Saint-Denis!*" *RN*, XII (1970-1), 447-57.

A common place-name, *Monjoie* derives from *Mons Jovis*.

192A Arnould, Charles. "De Petromantalum à Montjoie (Petromantalum, Mantula, Monjoie, etc. . . . .)." *RIO*, XXIII (1971), 1-16, 81-102.

Munjoie is from Gaulish *mant-*, "path", and *gauda*, "pile of stones".

193 Diament, Henri. "La Légende dyonisienne et la juxtaposition des toponymes *Montjoie* et *Saint-Denis* dans la formation du cri de guerre." *RN*, XIII (1971-2), 177-80.

The martyrdom of Saint Dennis is associated with *Mons Jovis* or *Mons Gaudii.*

194   Bugler, G. "A propos de Montjoie." *RIO*, 24 (1972), 1-6.
Mont, "mountain," plus the Germanic *gau(d)*, "region, place," gives *Montjoie*, "the area of a mountain or other elevated place."

194A   Rohlfs, Gerhard. *"Munjoie, ço est l'enseigne Carlun.* Querelles d'une étymologie." *RLiR*, XXXVIII (1974), 444-52.
Supports the derivation from *Mons Gaudii*, meaning a mountain from which pilgrims first see the object of their journey.

See also 104.

The only other single phrase to receive concerted attention is the formula *pleine sa hanste*:

195   Harris, Julian. *"Pleine sa Hanste* in the *CR." Essays Presented to Honor Alexander Herman Schutz.* Edited by Urban T. Holmes and Kenneth Scholberg. Columbus: Ohio State Univ. Press, 1964. Pp. 100-17.
The phrase signifies that the lance is recovered without harm.

196   Corbett, Noël. "Encore une fois *pleine sa hanste." RLiR*, XXXIII (1969), 349-52.
It refers to the force of the blow.

197   Mériz, Diana Teresa. "Encore une fois *pleine sa hanste." Romania*, XCIV (1973), 549-54.
"De sa grosse lance."

The synonym as a stylistic or lexical device:

198   Elwert, W. Theodor. "Zur Synonymendoppelung als Interpretationshilfe." *Archiv*, CXCV (1958-9), 24-6.
On adjectives of color in vv. 1979 and 485.

See also 206.

199   Meguro, Shimon. *"Roran no uta* ni okeru jakkan no ruigigo [Some synonyms in the *CR]."Regards: Furansu Bungaku Gogaku Kenkyū, Tōhoku Daigaku Bungakubu Furansu Bungaku Kenkyū Shitsu*, VIII (1964), 30-8.

200   Gougenheim, Georges. "Orgueil et fierté dans la *CR." Mélanges Frappier*, Vol. I, pp. 365-73.
Orgueil is pejorative, *fierté* neutral or positive.

201   Burgess, Glyn S. *"Orgueil* and *Fierté* in Twelfth-Century
       French." *ZRP*, LXXXIX (1973), 103-22.
       In the *CR, fierté* is primarily a feudal and military virtue; pride is only
       a part of its semantic field. *Orgueil* is pejorative.

Other words, phrases, and concepts:

202   Trompeo, Pietro Paulo. "Dulce France." *L'Azzurro di
       Chartres e altri capricci.* (Aretusa, V) Caltanissetta and
       Rome: Sciascia, 1958. Pp. 27-33.
       The expression has a different meaning now.

203   Lejeune, Rita. "La Signification du nom *marche* dans la *CR.*"
       Boletim de Filologia, XVIII (1959), 263-74.
       Contrary to the listing in both Bédier's ed. and Foulet's Glossary, *marche*
       means only "frontier region" and not "empire" or "province."

204   Simon, Hans Joachim. "Die Wörter für Gemütsbewegungen
       in den altfranzösischen Wortfeldern des *Rolandsliedes* und
       des Yvain-Romanes." Thesis: Erlangen, 1959.

205   Jones, George Fenwick. "The *CR* and Semantic Change."
       MLQ, XXIII (1962), 46-52.
       Value words often have ethical meanings which differ drastically from
       their modern counterparts and derivatives. The culture depicted is one
       in which the ultimate sanction for wrong-doing is shame rather than
       guilt.

206   Meier, Harri. "Ein dunkles Farbwort." *Wort und Text: Fest-
       schrift für Fritz Schalk.* Edited by Harri Meier and Hans
       Sckommodau. Frankfurt-am-Main: Klostermann, 1963. Pp.
       101-10.
       On the expression *teint fut e pers* in the *CR*, v. 1979. See also 198.

207   Gougenheim, Georges. *"Place* dans la *CR*: Recherche d'un
       contenu sémantique." *Bulletin des Jeunes Romanistes*, IX
       (1964), 1-4. Repr. in *Etudes de grammaire et de voca-
       bulaire français.* Paris: Picard, 1970. Pp. 306-10.
       Two meanings: "place dans une ville" and "espace de terrain" where an
       event occurs.

208   Hemming, Timothy Dominic. "La Mort dans la *CR*: Etude
       lexico-syntactique." *Heidelberg Colloquium*, pp. 90-4.
       Ocire is used for active, transitive meanings, and *murir* represents those
       with a middle or passive value.

209   Burgess, Glyn Sheridan. *Contribution à l'étude du voca-*

bulaire pré-courtois. (PRF, CX) Geneva: Droz, 1970.
Studies the change in literary vocabulary, focussing on the period 1150-60, but with many examples from the *CR*. A chapter is devoted to each of the following: *courtois, vilain, aventure, franc-franchise, honneur, proz-proece, bon, beau-beauté, gent, amour.* rev: Baldinger, *ZRP*, LXXXVII (1971), 142-7; Foster, *FS*, XXVI (1972), 492-3; Nichols, *FrR*, XLVI (1972-3), 143-4; For the meaning of *curteis*, see also 289.

210   Gougenheim, Georges. *"Compagnon* dans la *CR." Mélanges Le Gentil*, pp. 325-8.
Enumeration of usages, chiefly to designate R-Oliver and the Twelve Peers.

211   Planche, Alice. "Comme le pin est plus beau que le charme . . ." *MA*, LXXX (1974), 51-70.
Reflections on the pine in literature, and above all in the *CR*.

212   Popescu, Mircea. "Plorer des oilz (*CR*), llorar de los ojos (*Cantar de mio Cid*), lăcrămâ din ochi (*Miorița*)." *Congrès d'Aix*, pp. 473-84.
These and similar phrases have their origin in ancient incantations.

See also 122, 317, 357, 418.

VERSIFICATION

213   Lausberg, Heinrich. "Zur Metrik des altfranzösischen *Rolandslied." RF*, LXVII (1956), 293-319.
A study of meter in the light of the *Vie de Saint Alexis*.

214   Hall, Robert A., Jr. "Linguistic Strata in the *CR." RPh*, XIII (1959-60), 156-61.
Sound changes occurring between 1100 and 1150 allow the linguist to date certain laisses by their assonance and to explain some apparent contradictions as resulting from different periods of creation.

215   Monteverdi, Angelo. "Regolarità e irregolarità sillabica del verso epico." *Mélanges Delbouille*, vol. II, pp. 531-44.
Irregularities can often be explained as dialect developments, or, in the case of Franco-Italian, as effects of the addition of a new linguistic patina. Examples from *O* and *V4*.

See also 28, 123, 336, 356, 547, 573.

GEOGRAPHY AND TOPONYMY

Scholarly attitudes toward the place-names of the *CR* range from

Ménendez Pidal's view that the poet's depiction of geography is largely fanciful, to Prosper Boissonnade's attempt (*Du nouveau sur la CR*, 1923) to identify most of the poem's toponyms with places in Northern Spain. The geography of the *CR* as a whole has been treated recently only in an unpublished thesis:

216   Chédeville, Janine. "La Géographie de la *CR*." Thesis: Caen, 1967.

On Ch's movements and the site of the Battle of Roncevaux in the poem, see:

217   Burger, André. "Le Champ de bataille de Roncevaux dans la *CR*." *Coloquios de Roncesvalles*, pp. 105-12.
Exact correspondence between the geographical features and the details of the poem. Map and photographs.

218   Lambert, Elie. "Textes relatifs à Roncevaux et aux ports de Cize." *Coloquios de Roncesvalles*, pp. 123-31.
Texts relating to the use of the pass in the Middle Ages.

219   Louis, René. "Le Site des combats de Roncevaux d'après la *CR*." *Studi Monteverdi*, vol. II, pp. 466-93.
R died at Ibañeta, near the ruins of the chapel. The battle between Ch and Baligant took place on the Plain of Burguete.   rev: Menéndez Pidal, *CCM*, III (1960), 365.

220   Mellor, Geoffrey. "The Route of Ch in the *CR*." *BRABLB*, XXXI (1965-6), 167-76.
Identifies *Tere Certeine* (v. 856) as Cerdagne, *Nerbone* (2995, 3683) as Narbonne, *Galne* (662) as the old Roman town of Elne on the French side of the Pyrenees, and *Senz* (1428) as Saintes.

The identification of Nobles, whose capture is told in vv. 1775-9 and was probably the subject of a lost *chanson de geste* (104), continues to be problematic, with recent opinion leaning toward Dax:

221   Guiette, Robert. "Notes sur la *Prise de Nobles*." *Romanica Gandensia*, IV (1955), 67-80.
The narration of the taking of Nobles found in David Aubert's *Croniques et Conquestes de Charlemaine* (1458) identifies Nobles with Acs, present-day Dax. This same equation is made in *Gui de Bourgogne* and other late sources.

222   Rosellini, Aldo. "Noterella rolandiana." *SMV*, XX (1972), 193-201.
Nobles is not Pamplona, but rather *Ais en Gascoigne*.

223   Beckmann, Gustave A. "L'Identification 'Nobles = Dax'."
MA, LXXIX (1973), 5-24.

The waters which R uses to wash the fields in *CR*, v. 1778 are the thermal waters from which the name Dax is derived.

See also 474, 509.

Other studies on the geography of Spain in the *CR*:

224   Lambert, Elie. "Textes relatifs à Roncevaux et aux ports de Cize." *Coloquios de Roncesvalles*, pp. 123-31.

The R poet did not visit Roncevaux or the Ports de Cize, but the *Pseudo-Turpin Chronicle* does show direct knowledge.

225   Aebischer, Paul. "Les Graphies toponymiques *Sebre* et *Balaguet* de la *CR*, ms. Digby." *BRABLB*, XXVIII (1959-60), 185-209. Repr. in *Rolandiana et Oliveriana*, pp. 221-41.

Sebre, designating the river Ebro, entails agglutination of the medieval Catalan article *su* (*(ipsum*) (suggestion of Foerster); *Balaguet* can be identified with Balaguer. Both forms belong to the spoken language of Catalonia, and may testify that the author of *O* visited that region, perhaps in the company of the Norman contingent at Barbastro in 1064.

226   ——. "A propos de quelques noms de lieux de la *CR*."
BRABLB, XXX (1963-4), 39-61. Repr. in *Rolandiana et Oliveriana*, pp. 242-62.

Munigre (v. 975) is identified with Los Monegros; *Cordres* (vv. 71, 97) with Cortes; *Carcasonie* (v. 385) should perhaps be emended to *Tarassona* (i.e. Tarazona); *Tere Certeine* (v. 856) is Cerdagne.

Ferdinand Lot suggested (524) that the limits of the earthquake which precedes R's death (vv. 1427-30) coincide with the tenth-c. definition of *Francia* and thus represent an archaism. Laon as Ch's capital has also been regarded as an archaism.

227   Hollyman, K. J. "Wissant and the Empire of Charles le Simple." *AUMLA*, no. 8 (May, 1958), pp. 24-8.

The port of Wissant was not created until 950, and the name could thus not have served as a reference point in any contemporary description of the Empire of Charles the Simple (911-29). Vv. 1427-30 are therefore not an archaism.

228   Louis, René. "La Grande Douleur pour la mort de R." *CCM*, III (1960), 62-7.

Reviews the various hypotheses proposed for *Senz* in v. 1428. rev: Bertolucci, *SF*, V (1961), 316.

229   Lejeune, Rita. "Le Mont-Saint-Michel-au-péril-de-la-mer, la

CR et le pèlerinage de Compostelle." *Millénaire monastique de Mont-Saint-Michel.* Vol. II: *Vie montoise et rayonnement intellectuel.* Edited by Raymonde Foreville. Paris: Bibliothèque d'Histoire et d'Archéologie Chrétiennes, 1967. Pp. 411-33.

Vv. 152 and 1394 do not refer to Mont-Saint-Michel, but rather to Saint Michael under his aspect of the psychagogue. The toponym of v.1428 is the village of Saint-Michel at the Port de Cize, near Roncevaux.

230   Vinaver, Eugène. "Poésie et histoire: A propos de quelques vers de la *CR.*" *L'Endurance de la pensée. Pour saluer Jean Beautret, René Char, Martin Heidegger, Temps et Etre.* Paris: Plon, 1968. Repr. in *A la recherche d'une poétique médiévale.* Paris: Nizet, 1970. Pp. 201-8.

Laon is not an archaism, but rather results from stylistic choice.

See also 524, 553.

The geography of Saracen lands, especially of those mentioned in the Episode of Baligant, seems to have been fabricated from vague reminiscences and allusive connotations which have given rise to much modern speculation.

231   Labuda, Gerard. "Polska w *Pieśni o Rolandzie* [Poland in the *CR*]." *Roczniki Historyczne*, XXII (1955-6), 35-59. Résumés in French and Russian, pp. 57-9.

Puillanie, v. 2328, signifies Poland rather than Apulia, and could only have entered the *R* tradition in the eleventh c.

232   Reichenkron, Günther. "Zu den ersten Beziehungen zwischen Byzanz und den ältesten französischen *chansons de geste.*" *Südostforschungen*, XV (1956), 160-6.

Agrees with Henri Grégoire that *Jericho* (v. 3228) designates Oricos.

233   Sergheraert, Gaston. *De la CR au Capitaine Conan: Présence de la Bulgarie dans les lettres françaises expliquée par l'histoire*, vol. I. (Collection Mellottée) Paris: Editions de la Pensée Moderne, 1961.

CR: pp. 13-28. Mention of the *Bugres* in v. 2922 may derive from contacts with the tenth and eleventh-c. Bulgarian Empire. *La gent Samüel* of v. 3244 are the Bulgars, whose King Samuel reigned 977-1014.

234   Luka, Kolë. "Toponimia shqiptare në *Kagën e Rolandit* lidhun me disa ngjarje të vjeteve 1081-1085 [Concerning Albanian toponymy in the *CR* and its relation to certain historical events of 1081-5]." *Studime Historike*, XXI (1967),

no. 2, pp. 127-44. In Albanian with French résumé, pp. 140-4.
Toponyms which Henri Grégoire associated with Albania are supported: *Val Marchis* (v. 3208), *Cheriant* (3208), *Butentrot* (3220), *Jericho* (3228), *Canelius* (3238, 3269), *Malprose* (3253), *Baldise* (3255), *Val Penuse* (3256), *Malpreis* (3285), *Tere de Bire* (3995), *Imphe* (3996).

235 Noyer-Weidner, Alfred. "Zur 'Heidengeographie' im *Rolandslied.*" *Verba et Vocabula: Ernst Gamillscheg zum 80. Geburtstag.* Edited by Helmut Stimm and Julius Wilhelm. Munich: Fink Verlag, 1968. Pp. 379-404.
Identification of the pagan peoples in the *CR* is problematic, especially in the case of the *Avers* (v. 3242).

236 ——."Farbrealität und Farbsymbolik in der 'Heidengeographie' des *Rolandsliedes.*" *RF*, LXXXI (1969), 22-59.
Moral connotations of colors in the catalogue of Baligant's forces, laisses 231-3.

237 Hanak, Miroslav J. 'Torleus and Dapamorz. Two Examples of Ethnic Amalgamation in the *Song of Roland.*" *RF*, LXXXIII (1971), 405-22.
Both names result from a combination of historical reminiscences from different ethnic sources, mainly found in northeastern Europe.

238 ——. "Sven Forkbeard, Bjoern Ironside and the City of Iomsborg in the *CR.*" *Romania*, XCII (1971), 433-57.
Imphe is identified with Jumne. The orthographic difference is explained as a transposition or a mistake in transliteration. Vivien's historical prototypes would be Sven Forkbeard and Sven Ulfson or Estridsson. The *Terre de Bire* is the Land of Bjoern.

See also 28, 522, 523, 578.

PARTICULAR LINES AND EPISODES IN *O*

The items in this section are given in the order of the lines and episodes which they treat. For the most part they deal with literary interpretations, although matters of textual criticism unavoidably enter.

The Council Scenes

239 Roncaglia, Aurelio. "Sarraguce, ki est en une muntaigne." *Studi Monteverdi*, vol. II, pp. 629-40.
The apparent contradiction with geography is explained if one takes *muntaigne* as a calque on Old Spanish *montaña*, "land covered with shrub growth." rev: De Cesare, *SF*, III (1959), 461; Menéndez Pidal, *CCM*, III (1960), 367.

240 Burger, André. "Le Rire de R." *CCM*, III (1960), 2-11.

Defends the order of *V4* in the scene in which Ganelon is named ambassador. Literary analysis.

241   Wais, Kurt. "Rolands Tränen um Ganelon." *Australian Journal of French Studies*, VI (1969), 465-83.

The apparent inconsistency in the portraiture of R, defiant toward Ganelon in vv. 292 and 763, but defending him in v. 1027, is clarified through an examination of the textual traditions, including the non-French versions. An older state is posited in which R was not conscious of Ganelon's betrayal.

242   Schweitzer, Edward C., Jr. *"Mais qu'il seit entendud*: Ganelon's and Naimon's Speeches at the Council of the French in the *CR.*" *RN*, XII (1970-1), 428-34.

The speeches are more subtle than has been recognized.

243   Gibellini, Pietro. "Droit et philologie: L'ordre des laisses dans l'épisode de la colère de Ganelon dans la *CR.*" *Revue Romane*, VII (1972), 233-47.

O's order can be defended if one takes into account an observation of Pio Rajna on the survival of Germanic legal practices in the *CR*. Ganelon is ratified as ambassador by the collective decision of the Franks.

244   Capels, Kathleen M. "The Apple Incident in Laisse XXIX of the *Song of Roland.*" *RN*, XIV (1972-3), 599-605.

The incident is a calculated insult to Blancandrin and the Saracens.

See also 378.

245   Burgess, Glyn Sheridan. *"La CR*, Line 400." *RN*, XIII (1971-2), 165-7.

L'emperere meïsmes ad tut a sun talent means "[Roland] has the Emperor constantly in his thoughts." rev: Di Stefano, *SF*, XVI (1972), 123.

246   Kibler, William. "Again *La CR*, Verse 400." *RN*, XIV (1972-3), 621-3.

L'emperere meïsmes is the subject of the verb.

247   Lonigan, Paul R. "Ganelon before Marsile (*CR*, Laisses XXXII-XLII)." *SF*, XIV (1970), 276-80.

The seeming inconsistencies in this scene are the result of Ganelon's calculations.

On v. 485, see 198.

248   Harris, Julian. "How Old was Ch in the *CR?*" *RPh*, XXV (1971-2), 183-8.

The *CR* does not represent Ch as an old man, despite vv. 524-39 and 552.

249   Herman, Gerald. "V. 578 and the Question of Ganelon's Guilt in *La CR.*" *RN*, XIV (1972-3), 624-30.
Carles verrat sun grant orguill cadeir reveals Ganelon's resentment of Ch and betrays feelings which constitute a moral breach of a vassal's obligations.

250   Mellor, Geoffrey. "*R* 602 (*O: Puis si cumencet a venir ses tresors*)." *MLN*, LXXII (1957), 111-13.
Ses tresors is the subject of *cumencet a venir*, and *O*'s version of the line is to be maintained. rev: De Cesare, *SF*, I (1957), 467.

251   Levy, Raphael. "Interpretations of *venir* in *R* 602 and in *Perceval* 6428." *ZRP*, LXXV (1959), 342-6.
Supports Mellor's defense of the reading of *O*.

252   Johnston, R. C. "*Hoese* 'boot' in the *CR*, Line 641." *MLR*, LVIII (1963), 391-2.
An example in *Ruodlieb* of a box being carried in a boot reinforces the meaning of *hoese* as "boot", contrary to a conjecture of Dorothy Sayers.

For the naming of R to command the rearguard (vv. 737-82) see 323.

253   Ubieto Arteta, Antonio. "El verso 746 de la *CR.*" *BRABLB*, XXXI (1965-6), 331-2.
A curious note on the expression *vifs diables*.

On vv. 796 and 798, see 518.

On the conception of the Council, see 491, 582.

Charlemagne's dreams, vv. 717-36, 2525-69, 3993-4001. The main sources of controversy are their meaning (and in particular what they prefigure) and the sense of certain words designating animals.

254   Steinmeyer, Karl Josef. *Untersuchungen zur allegorischen Bedeutung der Träume im altfranzösischen Rolandslied.* (Langue et Parole. Sprach- und Literaturstrukturelle Studien, V) Munich: Hueber, 1963.
The visions are placed in the context of medieval dream literature and of other dreams in the *chanson de geste*. As a whole, they serve to reveal Ch's Christian duty. For the second dream (vv. 725-36), K.J.S. departs from the traditional interpretation that it prefigures the Trial of Ganelon, preferring instead to see it as a premonition of the Battle of Roncevaux. In general, Biblical and typological considerations predominate. rev: Jones, *MAe*, XXXIII (1964), 134-7; Györy, *CCM*, VII (1964), 197-200; Bender, *ZRP*, LXXXI (1965), 361-4; Jackson, *RR*, LVII (1966), 56; Horrent, *RPh*, XXIII (1969-70), 595-600; Von Richthofen, *Speculum*, XLV (1970), 332-3.

255 Braet, Herman. "Le Second Rêve de Ch dans la *CR*."
Romanica Gandensia, XII (1969), 5-19.
Criticizes Steinmeyer's interpretation. The dream foreshadows the Trial of Ganelon, as does the one which precedes it in the text. rev: Whitehead, *FS*, XXVI (1972), 181; Di Stefano, *SF*, XVII (1973), 109-10.

256 Richthofen, Erich von. "Las visiones del lebrel en la *Canción de Rolando* y el *Infierno* de Dante I, 101 ss." *Nuevos estudios*, pp. 103-9.
Brunetto Latini, passing through Roncesvalles, had a vision with elements similar to those in Ch's dreams, including the *veltre*.

257 Arinaga, Hiroto. "Kuma ka buta ka: *Roran no uta* no goku ni tsuite [Bear or pig: Concerning the vocabulary of the *CR*]." *Regards: Furansu Bungaku Gogaku Kenkyū, Tōhoku Daigaku Bungakubu Furansu Bungaku Kenkyū Shitsu*, XII (1970), 3-15.

258 Owen, David Douglas Roy. "Ch's Dreams, Baligant and Turoldus." *ZRP*, LXXXVII (1971), 197-208.
The fourth dream (vv. 2555-69) has been misplaced from its original position after the first two. The Episode of Baligant is the work of a late interpolator, Turoldus, who intervened after the work of the master poet. Critique of Burger's theories on the Episode of Baligant.

259 Whitehead, Frederick. "Les Rêves symboliques de Ch à la veille de la bataille de Roncevaux." *BBSR*, VI (1971), 156-7. Résumé. To appear in the Proceedings of the Oxford Congress of the Société Rencesvals.
A sensitive reading of the dreams as they relate to their context, leading to the conclusion that the first two prefigure the Battle of Roncevaux.

260 Braet, Herman. "Le *brohun* de la *CR*." *ZRP*, LXXXIX (1973), 97-102.
The *brohun* of v. 2557 is a strong dog and not a bear.

261 Hunt, Tony. "Träume und die Überlieferungsgeschichte des altfranzösischen *Rolandslieds*." *ZRP*, XC (1974), 241-6.
Sketches the possibility of four stages in the expansion of an original set of three dreams, anticipating only Ganelon's betrayal and his trial, into the four dreams present in *O*, developing an idea of D.D.R. Owen (258).

262 Van Emden, Wolfgang G. "Another Look at Ch's Dreams in the *CR*." *FS*, XXVIII (1974), 257-71.
The *ver(s)* of vv. 727 and 732 is probably a boar; the leopard of vv. 728

and 733 is Pinabel. The tact of the author of *R* lies in his refusal to interpret the dreams fully.

The Battle of Roncevaux

263   Györy, Jean. "Réflexions sur le jongleur guerrier." *Annales Universitatis Scientiarum Budapestinensis, Sectio Philologica,* III (1961), 46-60.
Interesting parallels between laisse 79 of the *CR* and laisse 120 of *Raoul de Cambrai,* in both of which the question of sanction through song occurs. *Li ber Gilie* of v. 2096 is perhaps a "poète-exécutant selon la technique orale," Gilles de Laon, whom the Oxford poet would have confused with St Gilles to whom the *péché de Charlemagne* was revealed. The *jongleur-guerrier* is largely an image of the twelfth-c. mentality.

264   Burger, André. "Les Deux Scènes du cor dans la *CR.*" *La technique littéraire,* pp. 105-26.
R's conduct is motivated by his pride in the face of Ganelon's threat, since in recalling Ch he would also be appealing for help to Ganelon. rev: McMillan, *CCM,* IV (1961), 88-9.

See also 68, 141.

265   Wagner, Robert-Léon. "Le Lieu et la personne (à propos du v. 1206 de la *CR*)." *Etudes de langue et littérature du moyen âge, offertes à Félix Lecoy par ses collègues, ses élèves et ses amis.* Paris: Champion, 1973. Pp. 599-608.

266   Holland, Michael. "Gautier et Margarit: Deux épisodes de la *CR.*" *CCM,* III (1960), 339-49.
The poet has Gautier return to Roncevaux from the heights in order to bring a new wave of Saracens to the battle. Margarit is allowed to escape death in order to place Oliver in the spotlight. *O*'s version of the two episodes (vv. 1311-19, 2035-76) is correct. rev: Bertolucci, *SF,* V (1961), 514.

For the episode of Margariz, see also 58, 59.

For the earthquake in anticipation of R's death, see 227-30, 524, 553.

267   Ruggieri, Ruggero M. "L'Episode d'Abisme dans la *CR.*" *BBSR,* VI (1971), 151-2. Résumé. To appear in the Proceedings of the Oxford Congress of the Société Rencesvals.
The Episode of Abisme (vv. 1470-1509) is an interpolation betraying ecclesiastical roots.

On v. 1682, see 574.

268   Locke, F. W. "Ganelon and the Cooks." *Symposium,* XX

(1966), 141-9.

The kitchen being associated with hell in the *De sobrietate* of Milo of St-Amand, Ganelon is a figure of the Devil. The episode (vv. 1817-29) is not comical.

On v. 1979, see 198, 206.

269   Picciotto, Robert S. "Marsile's Right Hand." *RN*, VII (1965-6), 207-8.

The incident is metaphorical, reflecting feudal relationships.

270   Aebischer, Paul. "Un Problème d'exégèse rolandienne: Maelgut, la conquête de Gautier de l'Hum (*CR*, ms. Digby, v. 2047)." *CN*, XXIII (1963), 146-52. Repr. in *Rolandiana et Oliveriana*, pp. 263-9.

Maelgut is Gautier's sword.

271   Jones, George Fenwick. "St Giles at Roncevaux." *FrR*, XLIV (1970-1), 881-8.

Hypothesis that the author of a Latin *geste* on Roncevaux, perhaps Turoldus, confused Egihardus with Egidius (Giles).

272   Atkinson, James C. "Laisses 169-70 of the *CR*." *MLN*, LXXXII (1967), 271-84.

The Saracen in this scene, whose pride R denounces, is the hero's physical and spiritual counterpart. rev: Mann, *SF*, XII (1968), 119.

See also 83.

273   Hackett, Winifred Mary. "Le Gant de R." *Romania*, LXXXIX (1968), 253-6.

The rendering of the glove (v. 2389) is not primarily a feudal gesture, but rather a recognition of wrongdoing.

274   Lyons, Faith. "More about R's Glove." *BBSR*, VI (1971), 148. Résumé. To appear in the proceedings of the Oxford Congress of the Société Rencesvals.

Supports W. Mary Hackett's interpretation with new examples, including one from a charter dated ca 1075.

275   Vinaver, Eugène. "R at Roncevaux." *The Rise of Romance*. Oxford: Clarendon Press, 1971. Pp. 1-14.

R's death scene as indicative of the transition from epic to romance. A reworking of part of 327. rev: Caulkins, *ECr*, XII (1972), 65-7.

For R's death scene, see also 328.

276   Zumthor, Paul. "Etude typologique des *planctus* contenus dans la *CR*." *La Technique littéraire*, pp. 219-35.

The *planctus*, a well-delineated motif in the *CR*, is best exemplified by Ch's lament over R, the poem's emotional climax. rev: McMillan, *CCM*, IV (1961), 90.

See also 399-401.

277   Vinaver, Eugène. "Note sur le vers 2900 de la *CR*." *Mélanges Lejeune*, Vol. II, pp. 929-34.

Conjectures *Cum en Espaigne venis a mal eür* or *Cum en Espaigne a mal venis eür*. rev: Joset, *MA*, LXXVI (1970), 536; Di Stefano, *SF*, XIII (1969), 319.

278   Herman, Gerald. "A Note on Verse 2900 of La *CR*." *RN*, XII (1970-1), 443-6.

In the line *Cum en Espaigne venis a mal seignur*, the *seignur* is Death.

The Episode of Baligant. Much ink has been spilled over the authenticity of this section, which has seemed to some to be inconsistent with the rest of the poem. Its dimensions differ with the critic's opinion as to whether to include Ch's third dream, which appears to foreshadow the Episode, or the *planctus* over R's body, which follows the first appearance of Baligant in v. 2614.

279   Aebischer, Paul. "Pour la défense et illustration de l'épisode de Baligant." *Mélanges de philologie romane et de littérature médiévale offerts à Ernest Hoepffner, par ses élèves et ses amis.* (Publ. de la Fac. des Lettres de l'Univ. de Strasbourg, CXIII) Paris: Société d'Edition "Les Belles Lettres", 1949. Pp. 173-82. Repr. in *Rolandiana et Oliveriana*, pp. 211-20.

The Episode allows Ch to win a judicial battle against another supreme lord. Marsile is insufficient for this purpose since he is only a vassal. The Episode de Baligant is thus "l'aboutissement logique du poème."

280   Ruggieri, Ruggero M. "De Baligant à Antea et de Roncevaux à Paris." *CCM,* III (1960), 79-86.

In the *Spagna in rima*, the *Fatti di Spagna*, and Pulci's *Morgante,* Baligant is presented before his battle with Ch as if he is a new character, although in all three he also appears early in the text.

281   Burger, André. "Remarques sur la composition de l'épisode de Baligant." *Mélanges Delbouille*, vol. II, pp. 59-69.

Turoldus wrote the Episode of Baligant, an integral part of his poem as can be shown by similarities between it and the rest of the *CR* in style, technique, and thought.

282   Garrow, Gloria. "The Baligant Problem: Review of Current

Opinion." Thesis: Columbia, 1964. *DA*, XXVI (1965-6), 2181.

283   Rindone, Rachel P. "An Observation on the Dating of the Baligant Episode in the *CR*." *RN*, XI (1969-70), 181-5.

The expression *Deus volt* in v. 3609 is a reflection of the crowd's answer to Urban II's call for the crusade in 1095.

284   Allen, John R. "On the Authenticity of the Baligant Episode in the *CR*." *Computers in the Humanities*. Edited by J. L. Mitchell. Minneapolis: Univ. of Minnesota Press, 1974. Pp. 65-72.

Preliminary results of a computer-aided analysis of the occurrence of high-frequency words show the Episode of Baligant differing from other sections. See also "Du nouveau sur l'authenticité de l'épisode de Baligant." *Congrès d'Aix*, pp. 147-56.

See also 105, 106, 124, 219, 232, 234, 235, 236, 237, 258, 307, 315, 319, 338, 344, 466, 529, 541, 542, 550, 568, 573, 576, 587, 609.

For Ch's return from Spain (vv. 3682-3704), see 77.

For the Episode of Alda (vv. 3705-33), see 66, 381.

The Trial of Ganelon. The indispensable work is still:

285   Ruggieri, Ruggero M. *Il processo di Gano nella CR.* (Pubblicazioni della Scuola di Filologia Moderna della Real Università di Roma, III) Florence: Sansoni, 1936.

The major work on law in the *CR*. Certain legal aspects, resembling most closely the Lex Burgundionum and Burgundian procedure, are evidence for versions of the poem dating back to the ninth c., of which Ganelon and the Trial were a part. All details of the Trial are compared to Merovingian, Carolingian, and Capetian legal sources. In a final chapter on the art and unity of the *CR*, R.M.R. interprets the poem as a *dramma della Fatalità*.

286   Halverson, John. "Ganelon's Trial." *Speculum*, XLII (1967), 661-9.

The accusation of *orgoill* is applied to R by Ganelon and the Saracens, never by Turpin. Parallels with *Beowulf*. In the Trial the view that loyalty is due first to oneself, then to one's lineage, and only finally to one's chieftain, is successfully challenged. While the "R part" of the poem reflects the old Germanic ethos, the "Ch part" (i.e. the Episode of Baligant and the Trial of Ganelon) introduces a new ethos in which monarchial prerogative is supreme.

287   Brook, Leslie C. "Le Forfait de R dans le procès de Ganelon :

Encore sur un vers obscur de la *CR.*" *Heidelberg Colloquium*, pp. 120-8.

Interprets provisionally *Rollant me forfist en or e en aveir* (v. 3758) in a figurative way as "R a nui à ma réputation, à ma valeur."

288 Charier, Jean. "*CR, 3795. Asez i ad Alemans et Tiedeis.*" *TLL*, VII (1969), 237-9.

On the preservation of the intervocalic dental in *Tiedeis.*

289 Burgess, Glyn S. "Remarques sur deux vers de la *CR* (vv. 3796-7)." *Congrès d'Aix*, pp. 63-78.

Rejects Jenkins' interpretation that the indulgent Auvergnats are responsible for Ganelon's acquittal. "De ceux d'Auvergne y sont les conseillers les plus sages. A cause de [l'intervention de] Pinabel, ils [les juges] se montrent plus enclins à la paix."

290 Hackett, Winifred Mary. "La Féodalité dans la *CR* et dans *Girart de Roussillon.*" *Heidelberg Colloquium*, pp. 22-7.

Thierry's arguments in the Trial of Ganelon depend on a conception of authority which is more characteristic of eleventh-c. England than of France.

See also 575.

The final incidents.

291 Keller, Hans Erich. "La Conversion de Bramimonde." *Olifant*, I, no. 1 (Oct. 1973), 3-22. Also printed in *Congrès d'Aix*, pp. 175-203.

Possible etyma for the Queen's name. Peter the Venerable's ideas concerning Islam influenced a hypothetical poet of St-Denis in his portrayal of Bramimonde's conversion. Laisses 239 and 290 of the Segre ed. would have been added by an Angevin *remanieur* under the impulse of the English cult of St Juliana.

291A Stranges, John A. "The Significance of Bramimonde's Conversion in the *Song of Roland.*" *RN*, XVI (1974-5), 190-6.

See also 391, 392.

292 Aebischer, Paul. "Les Derniers Vers de la *CR.*" *Homenaje a Dámaso Alonso*, vol. I, pp. 11-33. Repr. in *Rolandiana et Oliveriana*, pp. 191-210.

Two episodes, corroborated by the Danish *Karl Magnus Krønike*, are at the end of a version of the *CR* contemporary with *O*: the Libyan War and the Saxon War (*Baudouin et Sibilie*). Turoldus, the scribe of *O*, would have noticed that the ending of the poem he was copying was missing. Thus v. 4002 is to be interpreted: "Here ends the MS. of the epic which Turoldus is making accessible."

See also 568.

Ci falt la geste que Turoldus declinet.

293   De Cesare, Raffaele. "L'ultimo verso della *CR*." *Convivium*, XXIII (1955), 400-8.

The sense of *declinet* is illuminated by a letter of Anselm of Canterbury (after 1077) in which *declinare* is used to denote all the practices, exegetical as well as grammatical, of the medieval *lectio*. Other pertinent examples. Note 1 provides a bibliography to 1955. rev: Roques, *Romania*, LXXVI (1955), 555; Bourciez, *RLR*, LXXII (1956), 293.

294   Leblond, B. "Ci falt la geste que Turoldus declinet." *Annales de Normandie*, VII (1957), 159-63.

On the document treated in the preceding item, which the author does not seem to have known.

295   Christmann, Hans Helmut. "*Declinet* und keine Ende. Zur letzten Laisse des Oxforder *R*." *ZFSL*, LXXVI (1966), 84-92.

Reviews various theories. Both the word *decliner* (in the form *declin*) and an angel appear in laisse 178 and the final laisse. *Declin* also occurs at the beginning of Thomas' *Horn* and in *Amadas et Ydoine* with the meaning "ending".

See also 292, 528, 600.

AOI.

296   Lausberg, Heinrich. "Zur altfranzösischen Metrik: I. Das AOI des *Rolandsliedes*. II. Die Assonanz -*i* in den Refrains. III. Principien der Assonanzvokalwahl." *RF*, LXVIII (1956), 19-26.

AOI represents *Adonius* (i.e. Adonic line or strophe).

297   Louis, René. "Le Refrain dans les plus anciennes chansons de geste et le sigle AOI dans le *R* d'Oxford." *Mélanges Frank*, pp. 330-60.

AOI is a refrain chanted by the audience. rev: Benoît, *Provence Historique*, VIII (1958), 269-70; Muraille, *CCM*, II (1959), 479; De Cesare, *SF*, III (1959), 286; Benoît, *Flambeau*, XLII (1959), 378-84; Chambers, *RPh*, XV (1961-2), 80.

298   Mandach, André de. "The So-Called AOI in the *CR*."

Symposium, XI (1957), 303-15.
AOI is an error for *Am*, abbreviation of "amen". rev: Favati, *SF*, III (1959), 115; Bulst, *ZRP*, LXXV (1959), 550-1.

299 Crowley, Frances, and Cornelius Crowley. "Le Problème de l'étymologie de AOI dans la *CR*." *CCM*, III (1960), 12-13.
AOI is an abbreviation of "*a*insi soit-*i*l ". An alternative: from *adaudire*, "to listen".

300 Storey, Christopher. "AOI in the *CR*." *Essays Presented to C.M. Girdlestone*. Edited by E.T. Dubois and others. Newcastle upon Tyne: Univ. of Durham, 1960.
Agrees with René Louis in making AOI the symbol of a refrain, perhaps "H*a*lt s*o*nt li pu*i* ".

301 Miki, Osamu. "*Roran no uta* no AOI ni tsuite [Concerning AOI in the *CR*]." *Kansai Daigaku Bungaku Ronshū*, XI, no. 8 (1962), 1-13.
Brief summary of various theories.

302 Menéndez Pidal, Ramón. "El AOI del manuscrito rolandiano de Oxford." *RFE*, XLVI (1963), 173-7.
AOI is related to the ancient Germanic war cry "ahoy", used as an exclamation of exultation.

303 Devoto, Daniel. "L'AOI dans la *CR*." *AEM*, V (1968), 433-6.
AOI is a Basque war cry.

304 Green, Herman J. "The Etymology of AOI and AE." *MLN*, LXXXV (1970), 593-8.
AOI derives from the Greek *aoidos*, "bard, minstrel".

305 Mermier, Guy. "The *CR*'s Mysterious AOI." *Michigan Academician*, V (1973), 481-91.
Hypothesis that AOI represents *Alpha, Omega, Iesus*.

See also 97, 307, 585, 586.

See also Bédier's *CR commentée* (28), pp. 299-320, for comments on individual lines; and 47, 53.

V
THE POETRY

The study of poetic aspects of the *CR* (style, characterization, themes, structure, unity, comparison with other works) has supplanted to a large extent the preoccupation over questions of origins.

STYLE

Perhaps the most important single development in this area is the recognition that the *CR* shares a formulaic style with other epics, such as the Homeric poems and certain modern Yugoslav narrative songs. Some have claimed that this style is a sign of oral composition; others have seen in it only a mark of public recitation.

306   Lejeune, Rita. "Technique littéraire et chansons de geste."
       MA, LX (1954), 311-34.

   Studying the expressions *destrier abrivé, bataille adurée, destrier alferant,* and *Vivien l'alosé,* R.L. maintains that to examine the formulaic style from the point of view of modern aesthetics is inadequate, and appeals to the methods of Homeric scholars for enlightenment.

307   Rychner, Jean. *La Chanson de geste: Essai sur l'art épique des jongleurs.* (PRF, LIII), Geneva: Droz; Lille: Giard, 1955. Repr. 1968.

   One of the most important works on the *CR*'s style, dealing with ten *chansons de geste* dating to the end of the twelfth c. While the *CR* employs the same traditional means of expression (motifs, formulas, themes) as do the other early *chansons de geste*, it is extremely difficult to believe that it was orally composed. Masterful analysis of laisse structure. Other stylistic and organizational devices are also treated, including recapitulations, anticipations, and AOI. rev: Noy, *RFE*, XXXIX (1955), 389-400; Bossuat, *MA*, LXII (1956), 526; Peckham, *RR*, XLVII (1956), 117-21; Tyssens, *MR*, VI (1956), 73-80; Bonjour, *Romania*, LXXVIII (1957), 243-55; Ham, *RPh*, XII (1958-9), 87-91.

308   Lambotte, F. "Les Formules épiques dans la *CR*: Manuscrits d'Oxford et de Venise." Thesis: Louvain, 1959-60.

309   Lord, Albert B. *The Singer of Tales.* (Harvard Studies in Comparative Literature, XXIV) Cambridge, Mass.: Harvard Univ. Press, 1960. Repr. New York: Atheneum, 1965.

CR: pp. 202-6. Analysis of a sample shows that the poem is formulaic in style, and leads to the conclusion that the question of *remaniements* should be taken up again in the light of the theory of oral-formulaic composition.

310 Nichols, Stephen G., Jr. *Formulaic Diction and Thematic Composition in the CR*. (Univ. of North Carolina Studies in the Romance Languages and Literatures, XXXVI) Chapel Hill: Univ. of North Carolina Press, 1961.

On the basis of a study of formulas, enjambment, and themes, in vv. 1-2000 of *O*, the author concludes that the *CR* is composed in oral-formulaic style. The poet uses that style optimally and surpasses its limitations. rev: Hackett, *RPh*, XVII (1963-4), 819-20.

311 Fellmann, Ferdinand. *"Style formulaire* und epische Zeit im *Rolandslied."* *GRM*, XII (1962), 337-60.

Epic time as a shifting structural principle of unity.

312 Wathelet-Willem, Jeanne. "A propos de la technique formulaire dans les plus anciennes chansons de geste." *Mélanges Delbouille*, vol. II, pp. 705-27.

A study of formulas for the horse, weapons, and armor, which arrives at the provisional conclusion that formulas are flexible, that the *cliché* element resides in schemas, and that formulas originally were expressions occurring in the first hemistich. rev: D'Heur, *MR*, XX (1970), 119-20.

313 Hitze, Renate. *Studien zu Sprache und Stil der Kampf-schilderungen in den Chansons de Geste*. (Kölner Romanistische Arbeiten, XXXIII) Geneva: Droz, 1965.

Formulas for battle are analysed exhaustively. Fluidity in the use of past tenses is seen as a function of compositional technique. The existence of the earliest *chansons de geste* in oral tradition does not preclude poetic creativity. rev: Whitehead, *FS*, XXI (1967), 236-7; Singer, *Poetica*, I (1967), 576-7; Söll, *RF*, LXXIX (1967), 653-7; Friedman, *RPh*, XXII (1968-9), 334-6; Stefenelli, *Vox Romanica*, XXVIII (1969), 159-62.

314 Menéndez Pidal, Ramón. "Los cantores yugoeslavos y los occidentales: El *Mio Cid* y dos refunaiaores primitivos." *BRABLB*, XXXI (1965-6), 195-225.

Rejection of Parry's and Lord's theory of oral composition for the *CR*.

315 Holland, Michael. *"Rolandus Resurrectus."* *Mélanges Crozet*, vol. I, pp. 397-418.

Penetrating analysis of some principles of the *CR*'s formulaic style. Elements which constitute the laisse and the longer episode are submitted to a double fixity: that of the choice among possible details, and that of the order in which the details appear. Principles of composition are isolated which are equally at work in the Episode of Baligant and the rest of the poem.

316 Vance, Eugene. "Notes on the Development of Formulaic Language in Romanesque Poetry." *Mélanges Crozet*, vol. I, pp. 427-34.

Importance of spatial formulas in the *CR* and also of the formulaic viewpoint in *trouvère* lyric.

317 Wathelet-Willem, Jeanne. "L'Epée dans les plus anciennes chansons de geste: Etude de vocabulaire." *Mélanges Crozet*, vol, I, pp. 435-49.

The author of the *CR* may have been the first to attribute names to swords in the *chanson de geste*. Formulaic expressions dealing with the sword are used in a more varied and supple way in it than in other *chansons de geste*.

318 Jehle, Fred F. "A Study of the Formulaic Diction in the *Poema de mio Cid* and the *CR*." Thesis: Catholic Univ. of America, 1970. *DAI*, XXXI (1970-1), 2348A.

319 Duggan, Joseph J. *The Song of Roland: Formulaic Style and Poetic Craft*. (Publications of the Center for Medieval and Renaissance Studies, Univ. of California, Los Angeles, VI) Berkeley and Los Angeles: Univ. of California Press, 1973.

A computer-aided analysis of the *CR*'s formulas (*O*) in the context of nine other *chansons de geste* and three romances. The *CR* results from a tradition of oral composition, and is among the most formulaic of the epics treated. Includes studies of the formulas, their distribution in the poem, the Episode of Baligant, the relationship between traditional style and aesthetics, the motifs of the hero's death and the *planctus*, and ornamental formulas. rev: Heinemann, *Olifant*, I, no. 1 (Oct. 1973), 23-31; Lacey, *FrR*, XLVII (1973-4), 1172-3; *TLS*, March 29, 1974, p. 320; Nichols, *Medievalia et Humanistica*, new series, V (1974), 233-7.

320 ——. "Ha-epika ha-tzorfatit k'genre shel sifrut shenitkhabra b'al-peh [Oral composition in the Old French epic: A computer-aided method of formula analysis]." *Ha-sifrut*, IV (1973), 488-96. In Hebrew, with English summary, pp. xxv-xxvi.

Description of a method for determining whether the *CR* was composed orally or in writing.

321 Heinemann, Edward A. "Composition stylisée et technique littéraire dans la *CR*." *Romania*, XCIV (1973), 1-28.

Formulas used for aesthetic purposes. rev: Folkart, *SF*, XVII (1974), 519.

322   ——. "La Place de l'élément *brandir la lance* dans la structure du motif de l'attaque à la lance." *Romania*, XCV (1974), 105-13.

At the beginning of the extant tradition, the element *brandir la lance* was not an integral part of the motif.

See also 34, 85, 92, 128C, 263, 448, 530, 539, 559.

Along more traditional lines of stylistic analysis, an outstanding influence has been:

323   Auerbach, Erich. "Rolands Ernennung zum Führer der Nachhut des fränkischen Heeres (Laisses 58-62)." *Mimesis: Dargestellte Wirklichkeit in der abendländischen Literatur.* Berne: Francke Verlag, 1946. Pp. 95-119. Tr. as "R against Ganelon." *Mimesis: The Representation of Reality in Western Literature.* Tr. by Willard Trask. Princeton: Princeton Univ. Press, 1953. Repr. Garden City: Doubleday Anchor Books, 1957. Pp. 83-107. *Mimesis* has also been translated into French (Gallimard, 1968), Italian (Einaudi, 1956), and Rumanian (Editura pentu literatura universală, 1967).

A classic study. Parataxis is the dominant feature of *R*'s language, a new form of the elevated style dependent on the power of juxtaposed and independent verbal blocks rather than on rhetorical or periodic structure. In this style, the creation of vernacular poets, the realm of the heroic and sublime is routinely separated from the practical and everyday.

Auerbach is criticized in:

324   Battaglia, Salvatore. "I tranelli della *Mimesi*." *La coscienza letteraria*, pp. 129-44.

Auerbach analyses the *CR* in isolation from the broader medieval tradition and from the techniques of meter and recitation.

Other studies of parataxis:

325   Peeters, Léopold. "Syntaxe et style dans la *CR*." *RLR*, LXXX (1972-3), 45-59.

Demonstrates that parataxis is not a sign of primitive language, but rather a matter of stylistic choice. Among hypotactic constructions, Ganelon's discourse is the most complicated syntactically. Concluding remarks on how syntax serves the role of the epic in society.

326   Nordahl, Helge. "Parataxe rhétorique dans la *CR*." *RLR*,

LXXX (1972-3), 345-54.

Taking up some notions of Peeters, the author shows that parataxis can itself be a sophisticated device, particularly in conjunction with chiasmus.

Narrative movement is studied by:

327 Vinaver, Eugène. "From Epic to Romance." *Bulletin of the John Rylands Library*, XLVI (1963-4), 476-503.

The narrative movement of the *CR* consists of a series of loosely related scenes and gestures, largely devoid of temporal and rational links or transitions. In the romance both temporal and rational motivation are stressed. Remarks on the technique of *laisses similaires*. See 275.

328 ——. "La Mort de R." *CCM*, VII (1964), 133-43. Repr. in *A la recherche d'une poétique médiévale*. Paris: Nizet, 1970. Pp. 49-74.

The interplay between two movements, linearity and *entrelacement*, in R's death scene result in an effect which is alien to the modern concept of unity in a literary work.

328A Peeters, Léopold. "Le Présent épique dans la *CR*." *RLR*, LXXXI (1974), 399-423.

A three-fold movement (rising, caesural, descending) is seen as an organizing principle of the verse, the laisse, and the work.

Direct discourse:

329 Micha, Alexandre. "Le Discours collectif dans l'épopée et dans le roman." *Mélanges Frappier*, vol. II, pp. 810-21.

While it does occur in earlier texts, collective discourse becomes a significant stylistic feature only in the *CR*, where it is used 52 times.

330 Strauss, Dieter. *Redegattungen und Redearten im Rolandslied sowie in der CR und in Strickers Karl.* (Studien zur Arbeitsweise mittelalterlicher Dichter) Göppingen: Kümmerle, 1972.

The themes of the *CR* are transformed into narrative language consciously and systematically.

See also 449.

The Middle High German version is also used to illuminate *O*'s style in:

331 Hatzfeld, Helmut. "Le *Rolandslied* allemand. Guide pour la compréhension stylistique de la *CR*." *CN*, XXI (1961), 48-56.

O's virtues are stressed in the contrast.

Other stylistic studies:

332   Miles, Josephine. "The Heroic Style of the *Song of Roland*." *RPh*, XI (1957-8), 356-62.

The proportioning of parts of speech in the first 1000 lines, when compared to the same phenomenon in other epics, shows a strong favoring of predication, which is perhaps responsible for the tone of immediacy in the *CR*'s style.

333   Robson, C. A. "Aux origines de la poésie épique romane: Art narratif et mnémotechnie." *MA*, LXVII (1961), 41-84.

Three types of style perceptible in the Old English *Battle of Maldon* are also present in *O*. A study of the sequence of assonances would permit one to distinguish various steps in the prehistory of the *CR*. rev: Cézard, *Romania*, LXXXV (1964), 135-6.

334   Segre, Cesare. "Schemi narrativi nella *CR*." *SF*, V (1961), 277-83.

Affinities between the *CR* and evangelical style. rev: Lecoy, *Romania*, LXXXV (1964), 407.

335   Kvapil, Josef. "Problèmes de style dans la *CR* et dans la *Chanson de Guillaume*." *XII-lea Congres*, vol. II, pp. 621-7.

See also 29, 30, 36, 94, 598.

STRUCTURE AND UNITY

336   Knauer, Karl. "Un Aspect nouveau de l'unicité de la *CR*." *Langue et littérature*, pp. 257-8.

Résumé of research on the length of the laisse, carried out according to statistical methods and with the aid of a computer.

337   Robson, C. A. "The Technique of Symmetrical Composition in Medieval Narrative Poetry." *Ewert Studies*, pp. 26-75.

Sees units of 168 lines, or multiples thereof, in *O*, which would be tripartite in structure.

338   Farnham, Fern. "Romanesque Design in the *CR*." *RPh*, XVIII (1964-5), 143-64.

The poem's structure resembles a fivefold recessed panel arrangement such as is found in Romanesque altarpieces. This very suggestive article treats many other aspects of the *CR*, including unity, characterization, and the identity of the hero.

339   Martin, June Hall. "The Divisions of the *CR*." *RN*, VI (1964-5), 182-95.

The effective structuring of laisses in the *CR*. rev: Hicks, *SF*, X (1966),

115.

340   Nykrog, Per. "La Composition du *R* d'Oxford." *Romania*,
       LXXXVIII (1967), 509-26.
       Proposes a numerical structure based on groups of 1000 and 500 verses.
       rev: Di Stefano, *SF*, XII (1968), 325-6.

341   Vance, Eugene, "Spatial Structure in the *CR*." *MLN*,
       LXXXII (1967), 604-23.
       Spatial relations serve the poem's content and constitute an important
       aspect of technique. rev: Mann, *SF*, XIII (1969), 113.

342   Dorfman, Eugene. *The Narreme in the Medieval Romance
       Epic: An Introduction to Narrative Structures.* (Univ. of
       Toronto Romance Series, XIII) Toronto: Univ. of Toronto
       Press, 1969.
       R's death is a marginal incident and thus not a narreme, the sub-
       structure of the *CR* being the treason and its punishment. The structure
       of the Romance epic is found to be the sequence of narremes: 1. family
       quarrel; 2. insult; 3. acts of treachery or prowess; 4. punishment or
       reward. On this basis the *CR* and the *Poema de Mio Cid* share a
       common structure. This work has been severely criticized in reviews.
       rev: Scholes, *Philological Quarterly*, XLIX (1970), 137-9; Anderson,
       Lingua, XXV (1970), 205-10; Folkart, *SF*, XIV (1970), 123-4; Cotrait,
       BH, LXXII (1970), 171-9; Brault, *General Linguistics*, X (1970), 62-7;
       Kelly, *Speculum*, XLV (1970), 668-9; Crist, *FrR*, XLIV (1970-1), 812-
       14; Sturm, *Hispania* (USA), LIV (1971), 210-11; Utley, *Language*,
       XLVII (1971), 247-50; Fotitch, *CCM*, XIV (1971), 83-6; Ebel, *RF*,
       LXXXIII (1971), 359-63; Martin, *CL*, XXIII (1971), 362-5; Chaplin,
       BHS, XLVIII (1971), 58-60; Whitehead, *FS*, XXVI (1972), 55-6;
       Burgess, *MLR*, LXVII (1972), 413-14; Haymes, *CLS*, IX (1972), 92-3;
       Gumbrecht, *ZRP*, LXXXVIII (1972), 226-31; Grigsby, *Symposium*,
       XXVII (1973), 172-6; Damon, *RPh*, XXVII (1973-4), 240-4; Pei, *RR*,
       LXV (1974), 54-6.

343   Brault, Gerard J. "Structure et sens de la *CR*." *FrR*, XLV,
       Special Issue no. 3 (Fall, 1971), 1-12.
       The *CR* is structured in a double sequence of parallel episodes. Discus-
       sion of typology and the *fortitudo-sapientia topos*.

344   Bulatkin, Eleanor Webster. *Structural Arithmetic Metaphor
       in the Oxford R.* Columbus: Ohio State Univ. Press, 1972.
       O was composed on an arithmetical pattern discernible in the sequence
       of laisses, based on the number 66 up to the end of R's death scene, and
       on the number 91 for the remainder. Sixty-six is a combination of 11
       (symbolizing transgression of measure) and 6 (connoting evil); 91
       derives from 13 (Charlemagne) and 7 (completeness). The first of these

structures was imposed, along with the character Oliver, upon a previously-existing oral version around the year 1000. The second, with the Episode of Baligant, was incorporated around the beginning of the twelfth c. rev: Sargent, *FrR*, XLVII (1973-4), 976-7; Jones, *Speculum*, XLIX (1974), 98-101; Delbouille, *CCM*, XVII (1974), 160-2; Folkart, *SF*, XVIII (1974), 125-6; Hieatt, *MAe*, XLIII (1974), 37-41; Knapton, *RPh*, XXVII (1973-4), 428-36.

345   Van Nuffel, P. "Problèmes de sémiotique interprétive: L'épopée." *LR*, XXVII (1973), 150-62.
Notions of Greimas and Kristeva applied to the *CR* and the William cycle.

345A   Hunt, Tony. "The Structure of Medieval Narrative." *Journal of European Studies*, III (1973), 295-328.
An important discussion of recent work on structure, including 342 and 344. Many bibliographical references.

346   Niles, John D. "Ring-Composition in *La CR* and *La Chançun de Willame*." *Olifant*, I, no. 2 (Dec. 1973), 4-12.
The *CR* is organized by ring composition, an ABCBA type of structure capable of infinite extension. The miracle of the stopping of the sun is its centerpiece.

347   Mermier, Guy R. "More about Unity in the *Song of Roland*." *Olifant*, II (1974-5), 91-108.
The dynamics of the *CR* are provided by the continuum of spatially arranged actions in time. Comparison with the tympanum at Conques.

See also 29, 285, 307, 328A, 465.

CHARACTERS

Roland. The traditional view is that R is responsible for his men's deaths, since he failed to call back the main body of Ch's army when he should have done so. A number of recent interpretations have stressed, however, that R's conduct resembles the warrior ethos found in certain Germanic societies, and some would absolve him entirely of blame for the disaster of Roncevaux. The terms of this controversy were laid out in Alfred Foulet's article. Another controversy, akin to the first and now enmeshed with it, was occasioned by Alain Renoir's article and turns upon the question of whether the *CR* is primarily informed by Christian or by secular ideals. These are certainly the central interpretive issues of *R* studies, since the nature of the poem itself is at stake.

348   Foulet, Alfred. "Is R Guilty of *Desmesure*?" *RPh*, X

(1956-7), 145-8.

R places himself purposely in an untenable situation so as to ensure Ch's ultimate victory over Saragossa. Far from being at fault, R is right in his debate with Oliver. rev: Favati, *SF*, II (1958), 60-1.

349   Del Monte, Alberto. "Apologia di Orlando." *FR*, IV (1957), 225-34.

R is a martyr, Oliver a hero. R's refusal to sound the olifant is a super-human sacrifice; to have sounded it would have been merely human.

350   Renoir, Alain. "R's Lament: Its Meaning and Function in the *CR*." *Speculum*, XXXV (1960), 572-83.

Interpreting "pur mei" (v. 1863) as "through my fault", A.R. sees humble repentance in R's final stance. The poem is thus fundamentally religious in its idealism.

351   Whitehead, Frederick. "*Ofermod* et *desmesure*." *CCM*, III (1960), 115-17.

Emphasizes the differences between the *CR* and the Old English *Battle of Maldon* in regard to the hero's characterization.

352   Jones, George Fenwick. "La Complainte de R: Une interprétation divergente." *CN*, XXI (1961), 34-47. Tr. as "R's Lament: A Divergent Interpretation." *RR*, LIII (1962), 3-15.

Differing from Renoir, Jones maintains that pride is more a virtue than a sin in the context of the *CR*. There is nothing especially Christian about R.

353   Martins, Mário, S.J. "Evocação da *CR*." *Brotéria*, LXXV (1962), 294-306.

Retelling of the poem accompanied by an interpretation of R's struggle as essentially religious.

354   Moorman, Charles. "The First Knights." *Southern Quarterly*, I (1962-3), 13-26.

R not a tragic figure.

355   Owen, D.D.R. "The Secular Inspiration of the *CR*." *Speculum*, XXXVII (1962), 390-400.

The *CR*'s ideology is not religious but secular. R's conduct is governed by duty to king, country, family and self.

356   Hall, Robert A. "The Individual in Relation to his Society: the *CR*." *Cultural Symbolism in Literature*. Ithaca, New York: Cornell Univ. Press, 1963. Pp. 17-32.

In strata of the poem distinguishable on the basis of assonance, two conceptions of R are present: a saint-like fatalistic hero, and a foolhardy and insensitive one. Their combination raises the poem to the level of tragedy.

357 Jones, George Fenwick. *The Ethos of the Song of Roland.* Baltimore: Johns Hopkins Univ. Press, 1963.

Examines the vocabulary of moral and ethical concepts and of personal relationships, arguing that the pagan-Germanic ethos is central, although the poem shows traces of classical and Christian influence as well. In any case it is secular in its primary inspiration, contrary to the ideas of Alain Renoir, which are discussed in detail. G.F.J. rightly stresses that most modern translations render key medieval concepts inadequately, although he seems to eschew the use of the standard lexicological sources. rev: Adolf, *Speculum*, XXXIX (1964), 320-2; Györy, *CCM*, VII (1964), 65-7; Porter, *ECr*, IV (1964), 178-80; Payen, *CLS*, I (1964), 157-9; Woods, *Criticism*, VI (1964), 180-2; Burger, *MAe*, XXXIV (1965), 52-5; Guiette, *RBPH*, XLIII (1965), 1045-6; Walpole, *FS*, XIX (1965), 169-70; Hackett, *RPh*, XIX (1965-6), 117-20; Pérez Gallego, *Filologia Moderna*, XXI-XXII (1965-6), 163-4.

358 White, Julian. "La *CR*: Secular or Religious Inspiration?" *Romania*, LXXXIV (1963), 398-408.

Insists, with Renoir, on religious inspiration.

359 Walpole, Ronald N. "Le Sens moral de la *CR*." *TLL*, IV (1966), 7-21.

Curtius' *topos* of *fortitudo-sapientia* is absent from the poem. The true heroism of the *CR* is that of a conscience which learns to measure itself according to the demands of Christian morality.

360 Whitehead, Frederick. "L'Ambigüité de R." *Studi Siciliano*, pp. 1203-12.

The *CR* proceeds from Einhard's *Vita Karoli*. R's death is ambiguous, both a defeat and a victory, and the poet has not completely succeeded in merging the two.

361 Pearce, C. M. "*Desmesure* in the Old French Epic, with Special Reference to the *CR*." Thesis: Manchester, 1966-7.

362 Clark, Cecily. "Byrhtnoth and R: A Contrast." *Neophilologus*, LI (1967), 288-93.

The *CR* glorifies martyrdom, the *Battle of Maldon* the military ideal of the *comitatus*.

363 Cartier, Norman R. "La Sagesse de R." *Aquila: Chestnut Hill Studies in Modern Languages and Literatures*, I (1968), 33-63.

Not only is R free of *desmesure*, but he is the only hero in the poem whose wisdom and fortitude never fail.

364   Hieatt, Constance. "R's Christian Heroism." *Traditio*, XXIV (1968), 420-9.

Although R has much in common with Germanic heroes, he is without doubt a defender of Christianity in the poem. He is not guilty of the sin of pride.

365   Le Gentil, Pierre. "A propos de la démesure de R." *CCM*, XI (1968), 203-9.

R is guilty of egoistic excess in the expression of his courage, although his sacrifice has a higher significance, assuring as it does the triumph of Christianity. rev: Di Stefano, *SF*, XIII (1969), 319.

366   Payen, Jean-Charles. "La Geste de R." *Le Motif du repentir dans la littérature française médiévale (des origines à 1230).* (PRF, XCVIII) Geneva: Droz, 1968. Pp. 108-37.

R commits an act of *desmesure*, but it is not one for which he need repent. His is a *folie sacrée*. Cf. Frappier, *Romania*, XC (1969), 132-42.

367   Boatner, Janet W. "The Misunderstood Ordeal: A Re-Examination of the *CR*." *Studies in Philology*, LXVI (1969), 571-83.

R is perverting and destroying the feudal Christian ideal. He achieves self-knowledge through the humility of defeat.

368   Gérard, Albert. "L'Axe R-Ganelon, valeurs en conflit dans la *CR*." *MA*, LXXV (1969), 445-66.

The poem illustrates the passage from clan to national society.

369   Little, Edward Grant. "Epic Moderation: Structure, Narrative Texture, and Purpose in Heroic Literature." Thesis: Michigan State Univ., 1969. *DAI*, XXX (1969-70), 5413A.

370   Brault, Gerard J. "*Sapientia* dans la *CR*." *BBSR*, VI (1971), 144.

Neither R nor Oliver embodies the ideal of wisdom.

371   Donohoe, Joseph I., Jr. "Ambivalence and Anger: the Human Center of the *CR*." *RR*, LXII (1971), 251-61.

In their last encounter, R and Oliver undergo a reversal of roles, Oliver becoming blind and R gaining in moral vision. The characters are not "ideas in action" but rather mimetic representations of complex human behavior.

372   Kibler, William W. "R's Pride." *Symposium*, XXVI (1972), 147-60.

Orgueil is a grave sin, but R is *fier* rather than *orgueilleux*; his *fierté* is legitimate and praiseworthy.

373   Bloch, R. Howard. "R and Oedipus: A Study of Paternity in the *CR*." *FrR*, Special Issue no. 5 (Spring, 1973), 3-18.

Ganelon is the evil father who threatens and finally destroys his son; R is the son as rival.

374   Crist, Larry S. "A propos de la *desmesure* dans la *CR*: quelques propos (démesurés?)." *Olifant*, I, no. 4 (April, 1974), 10-20.

R's folly is the folly of God which surpasses human prudence. Critique, with a brief historical survey, of the idea that R is *démesuré*.

375   Van Emden, Wolfgang G. "'E cil de France le cleiment a guarant': R, Vivien et le thème du *guarant*." *Congrès d'Aix*, pp. 31-61.

Analysis of the concept *guarant*, leading to the conclusion that vv. 1864-5 are an admission of R's incapacity to fulfill the role of protector, and signal a change in his moral stance.

See also 240, 241, 264, 272-4, 286, 287, 338, 343, 421, 507, 559, 628.

Ganelon.

376   Louis, René. "L'Abbé Lebeuf et l'anecdote du chien Ganelon." *NC*, X-XII (1958-62), 207-14.

An eighteenth-c. anecdote concerning a dog named Ganelon who belonged to Louis the Pious may offer insight into the origin of the name and the time of the character's entry into the R legend.

377   Robertson, Durant Waite. *A Preface to Chaucer: Studies in Medieval Perspectives.* Princeton: Princeton Univ. Press, 1962.

CR: pp. 162-71. "In effect, Ganelon is not a human being, but an idea in action, a warning against the danger of personal malice." R's death is a Christian self-sacrifice. The *CR* is not a psychological drama but a moral tale.

378   Brault, Gerard J. "Ganelon et R. Deux anecdotes du traître concernant le héros." *Romania*, XCII (1971), 392-405.

The anecdote of the apple told to Blancandrin presents R as a diabolical tempter, while the anecdote told to Ch depicts him as an insubordinate vassal. rev: Stramignoni, *SF*, XVIII (1974), 126.

379   Beichman, Anthony M. "Ganelon and Duke Naimon." *RN*,

XIII (1971-2), 358-62.

Ganelon, by not volunteering for the embassy as did Naimes, leaves himself open for nomination by R, who thus exploits this procedural weakness.

See also 242, 244, 247, 249, 448, 450, 478, 576, 582, 628.

Oliver.

380   Favati, Guido. "Olivieri di Vienne (con appendice rolandiana)." *SF*, VI (1962), 1-18.

The earliest mention of Oliver in a document is from Savigny in Burgundy. Oliver was originally from Vienne, and thus a Southern French hero. rev: Faure-Alpe, *Bulletin Mensuel de l'Académie Delphinale*, VIII (1965), 164-8.

381   Aebischer, Paul. "Bavardages érudits sur Olivier, Aude et leur père Reinier, d'après les chansons de geste ayant Girard de Vienne comme protagoniste." *Mélanges Lejeune*, vol. II, pp. 709-37.

The characters Oliver and Alda first emerged in a version of the *CR* around the year 1000 and are the creation of the same author.

382   Battaglia, Salvatore. "Il 'compagnonaggio' di Orlando e Olivieri." *FR*, V (1958), 113-42. Repr. in *La coscienza letteraria*, pp. 91-128.

The companionship is an expression of the feudal fraternity in arms rather than of the classical *topos* of two faithful friends. The distinction *prouesse-sagesse* does not correspond to the Biblical *fortitudo-sapientia*, but is instead a result of contemporary interest in the problematics of heroism. rev: De Cesare, *SF*, III (1959), 286.

383   Herman, Gerald. "Why Does Oliver Die before the Archbishop Turpin?" *RN*, XIV (1972-3), 376-82.

Oliver dies as a warrior, Turpin while performing a Christian act. R's death is both the act of a warrior and the sacrifice of a Christian.

See also 344, 406, 555, 627.

Turpin.

384   Faral, Edmond. "A propos de la *CR*: Genèse et signification du personnage de Turpin." *La Technique littéraire*, pp. 271-80.

The *CR* is a militant work, written to encourage the crusading spirit, with Turpin as the ideal warrior-priest. rev: McMillan, *CCM*, IV (1961), 89.

385   Lejeune, Rita. "Le Caractère de l'archevêque Turpin et les
événements contemporains de la *CR* (version d'Oxford)."
Heidelberg Colloquium, pp. 9-21.

Turpin, symbol of the warrior-priest, is himself guilty of *desmesure
guerrière*. Two possible models: Odo, bishop of Bayeux, and Turold,
the Norman monk depicted in the Bayeux Tapestry. Abbot Turold and
Turoldus, the author of the *CR*, may be one and the same.

Baldwin.

386   Wais, Kurt. "Ganelons Sohn im Widerschein von Ganelons
Stiefsohn." *Studien zu Dante und zu anderen Themen der
romanischen Literaturen: Festschrift für Rudolf Palgen zu
seinem 75. Geburtstag.* Edited by Klaus Lichem and Hans
Joachim Simon. (Veröffentlichungen der Hugo-Schuchardt-
schen Malwinenstiftung, III) Graz, 1971. Pp. 207-11.

Reviews the relationship between Ganelon's stepson R and his son
Baldwin, who, according to late but perhaps archaizing testimony in
the *R* tradition, dies at Roncevaux in order to disengage himself from
his father's treason. The central conflict of the poetic legend is between
solidarity of the kin and faithfulness to the duties of vassalage.

See also 599.

Blancandrin.

387   Robertson, Howard S. "Blancandrin as Diplomat." *RN*, X
(1968-9), 373-8.

Supports the validity of the Blancandrin episode since that character's
role is logical and credible when his function as ambassador is under-
stood.

Gautier del Hum.

388   Lejeune, Rita. "La Composition de Gautier de l'Hum dans
la *CR*." *La Technique littéraire*, pp. 237-70.

Gautier is perhaps the celebrated Walter of Aquitaine, hero of the epic
Waltharius and of fragments of Old English and Old High German epic,
who had been raised by the Huns (thus *del Hum*). rev: McMillan, *CCM*,
IV (1961), 89-90.

389   Grégoire, Henri. "Le 'Gautier del Hum' de la *CR* n'est autre
que Gautier d'Aquitaine, héros du *Waltharius*." *NC*, X-XII
(1958-62), 215-17.

Supports Rita Lejeune on this question. In a "Note complémentaire,"

René Louis maintains, in addition, that Gautier entered the *R* tradition before Oliver.

See also 266, 270, 482.

Girart de Rossillon.

390 Coll i Alentorn, Miquel. "La llegenda de Girard de Rosselló i Catalunya." *BRABLB*, XXXI (1965-6), 73-81.

The name of the hero was included among the characters in *O* under the influence of the reputation of a young Pyrenean prince of the same name who fought in the First Crusade.

Bramimunde.

391 Brault, Gerard J. *"Truvet li unt le num de Juliane:* Sur le rôle de Bramimonde dans la *CR." Mélanges Le Gentil*, pp. 134-49.

St Juliana is a fitting model for the converted Saracen queen.

392 Domenico, Elio de. "Le due donne della *CR." Culture Française* (Bari), XX (1973), 17-21.

General appreciative remarks.

See also 291, 291A.

The Twelve Peers.

393 Vantuch, Anton. "Les Douze Pairs de Ch." *Philologica Pragensia*, I (1958), 6-10.

The peers are a clerical invention based upon Einhard's *plerique aulicorum* and the Saxon Poet's *palatini*. Only R and Oliver figure consistently among the peers in all *chansons de geste.*

See also 29, 35.

THEMES

Charlemagne's sin. A tenth-c. *Vita Sancti Aegidii* is the earliest text to mention an unspecified sin committed by Ch and forgiven through the intervention of St Giles (Aegidius), to whom an angel gave a parchment revealing details of the Emperor's conduct. The First Branch of the *Karlamagnús saga* and other vernacular texts specify that Ch had incestuous relations with his sister Gisela which resulted in R's birth.

394 Gaiffier, Baudouin de. "La Légende de Ch. Le péché de

l'empereur et son pardon." *Recueil de travaux offerts à Clovis Brunel.* Paris: Société de l'Ecole des Chartes, 1955. Vol. I, pp. 490-503. Repr. in *Etudes critiques d'hagiographie et d'iconologie.* (Subsidia Hagiographica, XLIII) Brussels: Société des Bollandistes, 1967. Pp. 260-75.
On the Latin sources of the legend.

395 Lejeune, Rita. "Le Péché de Ch et la *CR.*" *Homenaje a Dámaso Alonso*, vol. II, pp. 339-71.
Evidence of Ch's partiality toward R and of his prejudice toward Ganelon in the First French Council Scene of *O*. This and the mention of St Giles lead to the conclusion that the Oxford poet knew the legend of Ch's sin. rev: Kröll, *ZRP*, LXXVIII (1962), 598-9.

396 Lejeune, Rita, and Robert Escholier. "R était le fils de Ch." *Les Nouvelles Littéraires*, December 7, 1961, pp. 1-2.
General discussion of the legend, taking into account the iconographic sources.

396A Brault, Gerard J. "The Legend of Ch's Sin in Girart d'Amiens." *RN*, IV (1962-3), 72-5.
Girart d'Amiens' discreet version of the sin is seen as supporting Rita Lejeune's view that the Oxford poet knew the legend.

397 Sholod, Barton. "Ch and R: A Mysterious Relationship?" *BRABLB*, XXXI (1965-6), 313-19.
The legend of Ch's sin may have an historical basis, which would explain Einhard's initial reticence about R's death in the Pyrenees.

398 Bezzola, Reto R. "Les Neveux." *Mélanges Frappier*, vol. I, pp. 89-114.
Includes discussion of Ch's sin.

See also 104, 263, 271, 557, 599.

Death.

399 Frappier, Jean. "La Douleur et la mort dans la littérature française des XIIe et XIIIe siècles." *Il dolore e la morte nella spiritualità dei secoli XII e XIII: Atti del V^o convegno del Centro di Studi sulla Spiritualità Medievale.* Todi: Accademia Tudertina, 1967. Pp. 67-110.
On the *planctus* in the *CR.*

400 Brault, Gerard J. "Le Thème de la mort dans la *CR.*" *Heidelberg Colloquium*, pp. 220-37.

The representation of death owes much to the tradition of saints' lives.

401 Le Gentil, Pierre. "Réflexions sur le thème de la mort dans les chansons de geste." *Mélanges Lejeune*, vol. II, pp. 801-9.

The evolution of the theme, beginning with the *CR*, suggests clerical authors seeking to communicate an ideal of Christlike self-sacrifice. rev: Jodogne, *SF*, XIII (1969), 520; Joset, *MA*, LXXVI (1970), 534.

See also 208.

Biblical typology and religious themes. Many, although not all, of the typological interpretations which have enjoyed a certain popularity recently depend upon acceptance of the hypothesis of clerical authorship.

402 Bender, Karl-Heinz. "La Genèse de l'image littéraire de Ch, élu de Dieu, au XIe siècle." *BRABLB*, XXXI (1965-6), 35-49.

Ch the Elect of God appears for the first time in the *CR*, the Latin tradition remaining silent on this theme which probably developed under the influence of the eleventh-c. expeditions against Islam.

403 Mickel, Emanuel J., Jr. "Christian Duty and the Structure of the *R*." *RN*, IX (1967-8), 126-33.

Christian duty as a unifying element.

404 ——. "Parallels in Prudentius' *Psychomachia* and *La CR*." *Studies in Philology*, LXVII (1970), 439-52.

Analogies in situation, attitudes, dialogue, and descriptive attributes support the view that the theme of Christian duty is the unifying factor in the *CR*.

405 Ruggieri, Ruggero M. "Su alcune incarnazioni demoniache nella letteratura galloromanza e romena." *XII-lea Congres*, vol. I, pp. 1129-36.

The devil in, among other works, the *CR* and the *Ruolantes Liet*.

406 Rütten, Raimond. *Symbol und Mythus im altfranzösischen Rolandslied*. (*Archiv*, Beiheft IV) Braunschweig: Georg Westermann Verlag, 1970.

Prescinding from the question of genesis, R.R. reads the *CR* in the light of Biblical typology, with an admixture of various critical viewpoints: Mukařovský, Goldmann, Frye, Propp. Symbols treated include light, Durendal, Oliver's blindness. Among the myths are the crusading ideals, eschatology, and the myth of the Frankish state, a retroactive attempt to legitimize the Capetian dynasty. rev: Kelly, *Speculum*, XLVII (1972), 142-4; Whitehead, *FS*, XXVI (1972), 183-4.

406A   Meguro, Shimon. *"Rōran no uta* ni okeru 'kirisutokyōteki ky-ōi'[Christian marvels in the *CR*].*" Jimbun Kenkyū (Otaru Shōdai)*, XLI (August, 1970), 43-57.

407   Wendt, Michael. *Der Oxforder R: Heilsgeschehen und Teilidentität im 12. Jahrhundert.* Munich: Fink Verlag, 1970.

Analyses spiritual concepts in the secular epic and the question of ecclesiastical versus knightly inspiration in the *CR*.   rev: Wolfzettel, *ZRP*, LXXXVIII (1972), 221-6.

408   Vos, Marianne Cramer. "Aspects of Biblical Typology in *La CR.*" Thesis: Univ. of Rochester, 1970. *DAI*, XXXI (1970-1), 3524-5A.

409   Ward, Edward J. "A Study of Hands and their Association with Prayerful Attitudes as Seen in the *CR.*" *RN*, XII (1970-1), 435-42.

The author knew of various Biblical, classical, and contemporary literary portrayals of the attitude of prayer.

410   Noyer-Weidner, Alfred. "Vom biblischen Gottesberg zur Symbolik des Heidentals im *Rolandslied.*" *ZFSL*, LXXXI (1971), 13-66.

The symbolism of mountain and valley in the *CR* is linked to Biblical sources. Valleys have a diabolical connotation; that of mountains is ambivalent, ranging from the Christian *Munjoie* to the pagan Saragossa. The meaning of particular compounds of *val-* and *munt-* is treated.

411   Szittya, Penn R. "The Angels and the Theme of *Fortitudo* in the *CR.*" *Neuphilologische Mitteilungen*, 72 (1971), 193-223.

Michael is associated with R, who is endowed with *fortitudo*; Gabriel is the angel of Ch, whose virtue is *fortitudo Dei.* This contrast between the types of *fortitudo* is a major theme, brought into its sharpest focus in the horn scene.

412   Zimroth, E. "Grace and Free Will in the *CR.*" *Essays in French Literature*, 9 (Nov. 1972), 1-15.

Free will is conditioned by grace, which releases Ch from historical time and frees R from his depravity of will.

413   Brault, Gerard J. "Quelques nouvelles tendances de la critique et de l'interprétation des chansons de geste." *Congrès d'Aix*, pp. 13-26.

Various points of typological interpretation of the *CR*.

414   Vos, Marianne Cramer. "Portraiture de la haute royauté du Ch épique." *Congrès d'Aix,* pp. 83-107.

Asserts parallels between Ch and Old Testament kings.

Other themes.

415   Kahane, Henry, and Renée Kahane. "Magic and Gnosticism in the *CR.*" *RPh,* XIII (1959-60), 216-31.

Traces of gnostic influences, perhaps transmitted through Sicilian or Spanish channels, in the names of weapons, in pagan toponymy, in key Christian words (*Montjoie,* AOI), and in the name and character of Oliver. rev: Favati, *SF,* III (1959), 462.

416   Menéndez Pidal, Ramón. "Lo irreal y lo maravilloso en la *CR.*" *La Technique littéraire,* pp. 197-217.

Traits of fantasy occurring amid passages of strict logic are the product of a well-established literary tradition. rev: McMillan, *CCM,* IV (1961), 90.

417   Uitti, Karl D. "Poesía y visión política en la *CR.*" *Boletín Informativo del Seminario de Derecho Político* (Universidad de Salamanca), XXVII (1962), 3-25.

Ch's imperial mission, its idealistic and religious aspects, its fundamental anachronism.

418   Jones, George Fenwick. "Friendship in the *CR.*" *MLQ,* XXIV (1963), 88-98.

Amer is used in a non-emotive sense, signifying the formation of alliances or the making and keeping of the peace.

419   Nichols, Stephen G., Jr. "R's Echoing Horn." *RN,* V (1963-4), 78-84.

The horn as a unifying element.

420   Jones, George Fenwick. "El papel del beso en el cantar de gesta." *BRABLB,* XXXI (1965-6), 105-18.

Fewer kisses in the *CR* than in other works, and fewer in *O* than in the other MSS.

421   Bonnefoy, Yves. "Sur la *CR.*" *L'Ephémère* (1967), no. 4, pp. 55-65.

The *CR*'s substructure is based on the contrast between good and evil; its actions are caused by a mysterious fatality. R reinvents sacrifice, making possible his deliverance by breaking through the enclosure of the ego, the prison of being. The Saracens represent infinite, ever-regenerating evil. R's victory is in knowing that what saves man from death is the acceptance of death. Interesting interpretation by a major contemporary poet. See also 159.

422 Pountney, Catherine. "Le Portrait du chevalier dans les premières chansons de geste françaises." Thesis: Poitiers, 1967.

423 Frappier, Jean. "Le Thème de la lumière de la *CR* au *Roman de la Rose*." *Cahiers de l'Association Internationale des Etudes Françaises*, no. 20 (May, 1968), 101-24.
The contrast between light and darkness does not generally correspond to the opposition between Saracen and Christian worlds in the *CR*.

424 Nichols, Stephen G., Jr. "Poetic Reality and Historical Illusion in the Old French Epic." *FrR*, XLIII (1969-70), 23-33.
Poetic accounts of Roncevaux helped shape twelfth-c. awareness of the event. The poem offers an accurate picture of how the period viewed Ch's expedition.

425 Pellegrini, Silvio. "Il realismo della *Canzone di Rolando*." *SMV*, XVII (1969), 93-100. Repr. in *Ausonia*, XXV (1970), 11-18.
Defining realism as the presentation, in a concrete manner, of natural human situations, S.P. concludes that the *CR* is realistic, but not in the same sense as the paintings of Van Eyck or a poem by Dante.

426 Edmonds, Barbara P. "Le Portrait des Sarrasins dans la *CR*." *FrR*, XLIV (1970-1), 870-80.
General considerations.

427 Herman, Gerald. "Is there Humor in *La CR*?" *FrR*, Special Issue, no. 3 (Fall, 1971), 13-20.
Humorous episodes include Oliver's fighting with the stump of his lance, the words of Turpin in vv. 270 and 1484, Ganelon's ordeal at the hands of the cooks, and the destruction of the pagan idols.

428 Gajda, Daniel A. "Des jeux anthropologiques dans la *CR*." *Univ. of South Florida Language Quarterly*, X (1971-2), 19-22, 26.
Marsile's offer of treasure and hostages, R's offer of the apple to Ch, Ganelon's pact with Blancandrin, and Marsile's gift to Ganelon are seen as examples of potlach. Chivalry, jousting, and the ordeal are forms of game under the guise of warfare.

429 Kostoroski, Emilie P. "Further Echoes from R's Horn." *RN*, XIII (1971-2), 541-4.
In the second half of the poem, R's horn symbolizes his continuing

presence. Complements Nichols' article (419).

430   Kunkle, Roberta A. "Time in the *Song of Roland.*" *RN,* XIII (1971-2), 550-5.

Sees a seven-day division, reflecting the work-rest cycle. See also 455.

430A   Van Lent, Peter Cosby. "Love in Pre-Courtly French Literature." Thesis: Stanford, 1972.

431   Eisner, Robert A. "In Search of the Real Theme of the *Song of Roland.*" *RN,* XIV (1972-3), 179-83.

Ch and R are figures from a past age, but Ganelon reflects a disordered feudal world more contemporary with the poem.

432   Herman, Gerald. "The Battlefield Taunt: Violence and Humor in the *Chanson de Geste.*" *Annuale Medievale,* XIII (1972), 125-34.

Battlefield taunts are relatively straightforward and unsophisticated in the *CR.*

433   Uitti, Karl D. *Story, Myth, and Celebration in Old French Narrative Poetry, 1050-1200.* Princeton: Princeton Univ. Press, 1973. *CR*: pp. 68-127.

Dwelling on what he calls "binary impulses", K.U. shows how the *CR*'s poetic texture derives from the modulation of such dichotomies as the personal existence and the symbolic meaning of Ch, authority and being, Christian and Saracen, R and Oliver. Modulations are also observed at the level of the laisse. Sections on *Alexis* and Chrétien. rev: Crist, *Olifant,* I, no. 3 (Feb. 1974), 23-9;   *TLS,* March 29, 1974, p. 320; Nichols, *Medievalia et Humanistica,* new series, V (1974), 233-7.

434   Vance, Eugene. "R et la poétique de la mémoire." *Cahiers d'Etudes Médiévales,* I (1973), 103-15.

The oral epic discourse of the *CR* is a commemorative discourse by which the community of man living in history recreates itself in the light of a final Truth which inspires the incantatory word of the poetic performance.

See also 29.

COMPARATIVE STUDIES

French and Provençal works.

435   Schäfers, W. "Die syntaktisch-metrische Struktur des altfranzösischen *Wilhelmsliedes* und seine Beziehungen zum *Rolandslied.*" Thesis: Münster, 1960.

436   Owen, David Douglas Roy. *"Voyage de Ch* et *CR.*" *SF,* XI

(1967), 468-72.

Parody of the *CR* is a constant preoccupation of the *Voyage* poet, conditioning his presentation of the legend.

437   Patterson, Lee Willing. "Heroism and the Rise of Romance: An Essay in Medieval Literary History." Thesis: Yale, 1968. *DAI*, XXX (1969-70), 694A.

438   Muir, Lynette. "Est-ce qu'on peut considérer Vivien comme un anti-R?" *Heidelberg Colloquium*, pp. 238-44.

Contrast between Vivien's and R's death scenes.

439   Burgess, Glyn S. "Some Thoughts on R and Rodrigue." *MLR*, LXVI (1971), 40-52.

Both Corneille's *Cid* and the *CR* have a feudal framework, but *gloire* holds the place in the former which is occupied by *vasselage* in the latter.

440   Lynn, Thérèse Ballet. "Le *Jeu d'Adam*, la *CR* et *Yvain*: Une étude comparative des techniques et des traditions dramatiques." Thesis: Univ. of Illinois, 1971. *DAI*, XXXII (1971-2), 975A.

See also 290, 316, 329, 335, 345, 346, 558, 580, 618.

Spanish works.

441   Horrent, Jules. "*El Cantar de mio Cid* frente a la tradición rolandiana." *Coloquios de Roncesvalles*, pp. 189-209.

The *Nota Emilianense* proves that a version of the *CR* circulated in Spain, in the Spanish language, during the last half of the eleventh c. Neither the themes nor the style of the *Cid* originate with the *CR*, however, although several details indicate that the poet who composed the *Cid* was familiar with a version close to *O*.

442   Bělič, O. "La Conception du héros épique dans la *CR* et dans le *Poema del Cid*." *Philologica Pragensia*, I (1959), 3-12.

443   Richthofen, Erich von. "La Justice dans l'épilogue du *Poème du Cid* et de la *CR*." *CCM*, III (1960), 76-8.

The epilogue of the *CR* was influenced by the duel between Bero and Sanilo in Ermoldus Nigellus' poem on Louis the Pious, and in turn influenced the *Cid*.

444   Thomov, Thomas S. "La *CR* et le *Poème du Cid*: A propos de la question d'imitation." *CCM*, III (1960), 95-8.

The *CR* influenced the *Cid* in form and style.

445   Picciotto, Robert S. "Dramatic and Lyrical Unity in the *Cid*

and the *R*." Thesis: Indiana, 1964. *DA*, XXV (1964-5), 2966-7.

446 Battaglia, Salvatore. "Poesia e realtà nel *Poema de mio Cid*." *La coscienza letteraria*, pp. 151-69.

In the *Cid* events and characters are real; in the *CR* reality is invested with transcendent symbols —the Church, the Emperor, the nobles— more alive and enduring than real men. The morality of the *Cid*, an expression of everyday enthusiasms, contrasts with that of the *CR*, where moral values are a divine heritage. War is stylized in the *CR* but depicted without literary deformations in the *Cid*.

447 Thomov, Thomas S. "La *CR* et le *Poème du Cid*: A propos de la question des contacts littéraires romans." *Godishnik na Sofijskija Universitet, Filologicheski Fakultet*, LIX, no. 2 (1965), 337-69.

The *CR* influenced the *Cid* in structure, themes, descriptions of battles and juridical procedure, characterization, lexical borrowings. rev: Dembowski, *RPh*, XXIII (1969-70), 249.

448 Martin, June Hall. "Order, Morality and Justice as Traditional Epic Themes: A Comparison of the *Cantar de Mio Cid* with the *Odyssey* and the *CR*." *Southern Humanities Review*, I (1967), 274-82.

Combining oral-formulaic and Aristotelian categories, J.M. posits that the plot of the *CR* depends on the introduction of disorder in the person and actions of Ganelon. Ch is less deliberately committed to justice than the Cid, who must consciously seek it out.

449 Alonso, Dámaso. "El anuncio del estilo directo en el *Poema del Cid* y en la épica francesa." *Mélanges Lejeune*, vol. I, pp. 379-93.

The manner of introducing direct discourse is radically different in the two poems. rev: Joset, *MA*, LXXVI (1970), 524-5.

See also 318, 342.

Germanic literature.

450 Zink, Georges. "Chansons de geste et épopées allemandes: Deux contributions à l'étude de leurs rapports. 1. Sibeche et Ganelon. 2. Le récit d'une expédition guerrière dans le *Chant d'Annon*." *Etudes Germaniques*, XVII (1962), 125-36.

Two instances of possible Germanic influence on the *CR*

451 Renoir, Alain. "The Heroic Oath in *Beowulf*, the *CR*, and the *Nibelungenlied*." *Studies in Old English Literature in*

Honor of Arthur G. Brodeur. Edited by Stanley B.
Greenfield. Eugene, Oregon: Univ. of Oregon Press, 1963.
Pp. 237-66.

A finely nuanced comparison of the heroic oath as the principal source
of action in the three greatest secular epics of the Middle Ages.

For comparisons with the *Battle of Maldon*, see 333, 351, 362.

Dante.

452   Ruggieri, Ruggero M. "Etude comparative des significations
et des métamorphoses d'un *topos* chevaleresque dans la
Divine Comédie et dans la *CR.*" *Langue et littérature*,
pp. 394-5.

Common attitude in the two poems toward prowess and courtliness.

453   ——. "Tradizione e originalità nel lessico 'cavalleresco' di
Dante: Dante e la *CR.*" *Romania: Scritti offerti a Francesco
Piccolo nel suo LXX compleanno.* Naples: Armanni, 1962.
Pp. 427-50.

The contrast in Dante between *cortesia-valore* and *orgoglio-dismisura* is
analogous to the opposition Oliver-R.

454   Hardie, Colin Graham. "The *Veltres* in the *CR* and Dante's
Veltro." *Deutsches Dante Jahrbuch*, XLI-XLII (1964),
158-72.

Parallels in regard to poetic dreams and their fulfillment. Dante had
read the *CR*.

The Romance epic.

455   Pollmann, Leo. *Das Epos in den romanischen Literaturen:
Verlust und Wandlungen.* (Sprache und Literatur, XXXIV)
Stuttgart: Kohlhammer, 1966.

The *CR* is treated on pp. 13-36. L.P. posits categories of verticality and
horizontality for the Romance epic, the *CR* embodying the latter. Also
treated are time, the autonomy of parts, ideology. rev: Schulze, *RF*,
LXXX (1968), 449-52.

Other comparative studies.

456   Farahmand, M. "Le *Shahnameh* et la *CR*: Etude sur certains
points de contact entre la *CR* et l'épisode de Siavash dans le
Livre des Rois." Thesis: Paris, 1961.

457   Petriconi, Hellmuth. "Der Tod des Helden." *Metamorphosen*

der Träume: Fünf Beispiele zu einer Literaturgeschichte als Themengeschichte. Frankfurt am Main: Athenäum, 1971. Pp. 115-58. The section dealing with the *CR* is a reprint of "R, Don Quijote und Simson." *RJ*, XII (1961), 209-28. *CR* used as an example.

458   Etiemble, René. "Mest'fa Ben Brāhīm et Turoldus, Gésar et R." *Littérature savante et littérature populaire: Bardes, conteurs, écrivains. Actes du sixième Congrès National de la Société Française de Littérature Comparée (Rennes: 23-25 Mai 1963).* Paris: Didier, 1965. Pp. 40-53.
A Tibetan hero and an Algerian bard shed light on the *CR*.

459   Satō, Teruo. "Le Pathétique dans la *CR* et dans le *Heike-Monogatari*." *BRABLB*, XXXI (1965-6), 273-93.
Kiso's death is pathetic by suggestion and is without hope, whereas R's is directly pathetic and at the same time triumphant.

460   ——· "Chūsei senki bungaku no futatsu no heikōsen: Furansu to nippon no baai, I [Two parallel examples of medieval epic literature: France and Japan, I]." *Waseda Daigaku Daigakuin Bungaku Kenkyūka Kiyō*, XII (1966), 73-97.
Considers the *chansons de geste*, and in particular the *CR*, as essentially different from other medieval European epic literature in their relation to history, and akin to the Japanese medieval epic.

461   Thomas, Paul. "Cathédrales de mouvement et de lumière: Etude comparative de l'esthétique visuelle dans la chanson de geste et au cinéma (à propos de la *CR* et de *Raoul de Cambrai*)." Thesis: Caen, 1968.

462   Aebischer, Paul. "Arnold de Winkelried, le héros de Sempach et R, le vainqueur de Roncevaux: Observations sur la technique du montage, du lancement et de la mise en orbite de quelques mythes dans le cosmos historico-littéraire." *RSH*, XIX (1969), 1-33.
While the presence of the two heroes at the respective historical events cannot be established beyond doubt, they illustrate the process through which history incorporates myth.

463   Bluh, Frances Adele. "The Presentation and Destruction of the Kingdom: A Study of *Sir Orfeo, La CR, Morte Arthure,* and *Le Morte Arthur*." Thesis: Yale, 1972. *DAI*, XXXIII (1972-3), 6899A-6900A.

464   Minis, Cola. "Stilelemente in der Kreuzzugschronik des

Albert von Aachen und in der volkssprachigen Epik, besonders in der *CR.*" *Literatur und Sprache im europäischen Mittelalter: Festschrift für Karl Langosch zum 70. Geburtstag.* Edited by Alf Önnerfors, Johannes Rathofer, and Fritz Wagner. Darmstadt: Wissenschaftliche Buchgesellschaft, 1973. Pp. 356-63.

465   Satō, Teruo. *Rōran no uta to Heike Monogatari —hikaku kenkyū* [The *CR* and the *Heike Monogatari* —a comparative study]. 2 vols. Tokyo: Chūō Kōron Sha, 1973.

Reviews the *CR*'s MS tradition, discusses the Battle of Roncevaux and the legend's growth, and establishes a three-part comparison: structure, the theme of pathos, and descriptive techniques.   rev: Tomikura, *Bungaku*, XLII, no. 5 (May, 1974), 125-30.

466   Knapp, F. P. "Die grosse Schlacht zwischen Orient und Okzident in der abendlandischen Epik: Ein antikes Thema in mittelalterlichen Gewand." *GRM*, XXV (1974), 129-52.

Places the Episode of Baligant in the epic tradition.

467   Paquette, Jean-Marcel. "Epopée et roman: Continuité ou discontinuité?" *Etudes Littéraires*, IV (1971), 9-38.

See also 404, 558.

THE *CHANSON DE ROLAND* IN HISTORY

Myths of genesis preoccupied nineteenth-century historiographers, literary historians among them. Exceedingly little is known either about the defeat of Ch's rearguard in the campaign of 778 or about the state of the *CR* prior to *O*, with the result that the early history of the R legend has long been the object of prolific speculation and has been particularly vulnerable to nationalistic interpretations. The theories which attracted most attention and elicited the most controversy before 1955 were in the area which is the subject of this chapter. Since scholarship has continued to be divided along lines first established in 1908, or on some points even earlier, I have included the classic treatments of origins in cases where they still retain an interest for modern studies.

THE ORIGINAL HISTORICAL EVENTS

Carolingian historical works are the principal source for knowledge of Ch's expedition to Spain. The earliest of these include annals of an official or semi-official nature, the *Chronicle of Moissac*, the *Vita Karoli* of Einhard (Eginhard), an official at Ch's court and secretary to his successor Louis the Pious, the *Vita Hludowici imperatoris* by the writer known as the Limousin Astronomer, and the works of the Saxon poet and the Monk of Saint Gall, dating in the main from the ninth c. Einhard is the first to mention an historical R, killed by the *Wascones* (either Gascons or Basques) as Ch's army returned across the Pyrenees, but the question of R's existence is clouded by the fact that only one family of the MSS of Einhard's *Vita* includes the words *et Hruodlandus Brittannici limitis praefectus*, the sole reference in a written source to R before the eleventh c. (but see item 485). A phrase in the Limousin Astronomer's account (dated *ca* 842) has also given rise to much discussion: the chronicler explicitly omits the names of those who fell in the skirmish: *quorum, quia volgata sunt, nomina dicere supersedi.* Depending on the connotation attached to the word *volgata* (see 543, 548), scholars have sometimes taken this as an indication that songs about the battle were circulating already in the ninth c. Writing in the year 908, the chronicler Reginon claims to have based his account on a *libello plebeio et rusticano* as well as on the narratives of old men. A succinct account of the Carolingian sources and quotation of the pertinent passages, although from a distinctly conservative point of view, is found in the article by Silvio Pellegrini (476).

In addition to Carolingian historiographers, three other important sources are available: the Latin epitaph of Ch's seneschal Eggihard which furnishes the date of August 15, 778 for the destruction of the rearguard, various Arabic chronicles whose relevant passages are included in the Appendix to Menéndez Pidal's book (541-2), and finally numismatic evidence.

468 Thompson, J. W. "The Manuscripts of Einhard's *Vita Karoli* and the Matter of R." *Mélanges offerts à Henri Pirenne.* Brussels: Vromant, 1926. Vol. I, pp. 519-32.

The words *et Hruodlandus Brittannici limitis praefectus* were added to one group of MSS by Einhard himself in the third decade of the ninth c.

469 Abadal, Ramón de. "La expedición de Carlomagno a Zaragoza: El hecho histórico, su carácter y su significación." *Coloquios de Roncesvalles*, pp. 39-71.

After a review of all available sources, the author concludes that Ibn al-Arabi's sons did not attack Ch's army in the Pyrenees, but rather between the river Ebro and Pamplona. The Pyrenean ambush was carried out by Gascons, subjects of Lupus. Ch's initial motivation for the expedition was both political and religious.

470 Frank, István. "L'Affaire de Roncevaux, 778-1953." *Coloquios de Roncesvalles*, pp. 212-28.

In calling upon his personal knowledge to tell about the defeat of Ch's rearguard, Einhard was imitating Suetonius. The only incontrovertible fact concerning the poem's origin is that R owes his literary existence to the poet. In a note added after the discovery of the *Nota Emilianense* (486), I.F. calls for a re-examination of Bédier's theories and for archeological studies of the Valley of Roncevaux.

471 Lejeune, Rita. "Localisation de la défaite de Ch aux Pyrénées en 778, d'après les chroniqueurs carolingiens." *Coloquios de Roncesvalles*, pp. 73-103.

The defeat took place near the Perthus. rev: Roques, *Romania*, LXXVII (1956), 283.

472 Aebischer, Paul. "L'Expédition de Ch en Espagne jusqu'à la

bataille de Roncevaux." *RSH*, VII (1957), 28-43. Repr. in
Rolandiana et Oliveriana, pp. 83-98.
The Spanish campaign was poorly planned and carried out. rev: Roques,
Romania, LXXVIII (1957), 283.

473   Menéndez Pidal, Ramón. "Roncesvalles: El suceso histórico."
Novedades Editoriales Españolas, XV (1957), 41-8.
A treatment of the event from the point of view both of Arabic
historians and of the official Carolingian historiographers.

474   Aebischer, Paul. "Le Rôle de Pampelune lors de l'expédition
franque de 778 en Espagne d'après l'histoire et l'épique
médiévale." *RSH*, IX (1959), 305-33.
Agrees with d'Abadal that the Wascones of Einhard's account are
Gascons. Nobles is Pamplona and not Dax.

475   Ubieto Arteta, Antonio. "La derrota de Carlomagno y la
CR." *Hispania, Revista Española de Historia*, XXII (1963),
3-28.
The battle may have taken place at Siresa (province of Huesca). rev:
De Cesare, *SF*, VIII (1964), 315; Goyhénèche, *AMi*, LXXVI (1964),
105-6.

476   Pellegrini, Silvio. "La campagna del 778 nella tradizione
storiografica fino al secolo X." *Studi rolandiani*, pp. 27-74.
Review and critique of Carolingian sources.

477   Aebischer, Paul. "R: Mythe ou personnage historique?"
RBPH, XLIII (1965), 849-901. Repr. in *Rolandiana et
Oliveriana*, pp. 99-138.
Proofs alleged for the existence of an historical R are insufficient. The R
whose name is found on a Carolingian coin is probably that of the coiner
and not of the Count of Brittany. rev: De Cesare, *SF*, X (1966), 319.

478   Gibbs, Jack. "La Bataille de Roncevaux dans *Los anales de
España* de don Joseph Pellicer (1681)." *BRABLB*, XXXI
(1965-6), 99-104.
Inspired by Pellicer's account, J.G. maintains that the defeat was caused
by a tactical error on Ch's part. Ganelon was a traditional name for
traitors before *O*.

479   Aebischer, Paul. "Les Vainqueurs de la bataille des
Pyrénées du 15 août 778: Basques ou Gascons?" *Mélanges
offerts à M. Georges Bonnard à l'occasion de son quatre-
vingtième anniversaire.* (Univ. de Lausanne, Publ. de la Fac.
de Philosophie et Lettres, XVIII) Geneva: Droz, 1966. Pp.

161-78.

Gascons defeated Ch's rearguard, without help from the Arabs, who had already rescued Ibn al-Arabi, perhaps near the passes of Carrascal and Uznué 20 kilometers south of Pamplona.

480 Louis, René. "A propos de l'épitaphe métrique d'Eggihard, sénéschal de Ch." *Studi Siciliano*, pp. 685-710.

Diplomatic and reconstructed ed., with commentary. Remarks on why R, and not Eggihard, was the subject of songs.

481 Lacarra, José María. "A propos de la route de Roncevaux et du lieu de la bataille." *AMi*, LXXVIII (1966), 377-89.

Ch's army used the pass of Roncevaux-Cize in crossing the Pyrenees, so that the battle could not have taken place at Siresa.

482 Ross, D. J. A. "Gautier del Hum, an Historical Element in the *CR*?" *MLR*, LXI (1966), 409-15.

The battle may have taken place near the Pass of Lepoeder.

483 Horrent, Jules. "La Bataille des Pyrénées de 778." *MA*, LXXVIII (1972), 197-227.

The mention of *Hruodlandus* in Einhard, the *Rodlandus* of the Carolingian coins, and the *Rothlandus* in the document of Lorsch are all authentic references to an historical R, Prefect of the March of Brittany. See also 571.

483A Volkova, Z. N. "Znachenie arabskikh khronik dlia opredeleniia genezisa *Pesni o Rolande* [The significance of Arabic chronicles for the study of the genesis of the *CR*]." *Narody Azii i Afriki* (Moscow), (1972), no. 4, pp. 140-5.

484 Horrent, Jules. "L'Equipée espagnole de Ch en 778 avant et après la bataille des Pyrénées." *Mélanges Le Gentil*, pp. 377-98.

Ch's expedition was not a crusade, nor was the attack on the rearguard carried out by Basques and Arabs in collusion. The Spanish campaign was abandoned on account of the unstable political situation in Aquitaine.

See also 29, 36, 50, 465, 541, 542, 557, 559, 561, 562, 565, 567, 568.

Numismatics. Two coins bearing on the obverse the name *Carlus* and on the reverse the name *Rōdlan*, have been discovered, the first at Imply near Nevers in 1858, the second near Ilanz by the ruins of the castle of Grüneck in Switzerland in 1904. If the *Rodlan(dus)* in question is a Count of the March, charged with supervision of coinage, and not merely a moneyer, he could well be the R mentioned by Einhard.

485   Stiennon, Jacques. "Le Denier de Ch au nom de R." *CCM*, III (1960), 87-95.

Rôdlan is indeed the same person as the *Hruodlandus* of Einhard. rev: Lafaurie, *Revue de Numismatique*, III (1961), 246.

See also 483, 568.

THE *NOTA EMILIANENSE*

A short note written on a page of MS. 39 of the Real Academia de la Historia in Madrid recounts an archaic version of the legend of Roland. This note is the oldest extant version of the legend, and the first text to name Roncevaux as the place of battle.

486   Alonso, Dámaso. "La primitiva épica francesa a la luz de una Nota Emilianense." *RFE*, XXXVII (1953), 1-94. Repr. in *Primavera temprana de la literatura europea.* (Colección Guadarrama de Crítica y Ensayo, XXII) Madrid: Guadarrama, 1961. Pp. 81-200. Also repr. in *Obras completas,* Vol. II. *Estudios y ensayos sobre literatura.* 1ª parte. *Desde los orígenes románicos hasta finales del siglo XVI.* Madrid: Gredos, 1973. Pp. 225-319.

An account of the *Nota Emilianense*'s discovery by Dámaso Alonso. Written in Visigothic hand by a scribe whom D.A. identifies as having worked from 1048 to 1070, the note summarizes a version of the legend without Ganelon's treachery. It proves that a poetic tale about R circulated, probably in Spanish, in the third quarter of the eleventh c.

487   Walpole, Ronald N. "The *Nota Emilianense*: New Light (but How Much?) on the Origins of the Old French Epic." *RPh*, X (1956-7), 1-18.

The *Nota* may be contemporary with *O* rather than earlier. Scepticism about the pairing of heroes' names in eleventh-c. charters, about the presence of *fortitudo-sapientia* in *O*, and about the *Fragment of the Hague* as evidence for a poetic tradition. rev: Favati, *SF*, I (1957), 467; Aubert, *RHE*, LIII (1958), 638.

488   Menéndez Pidal, Gonzalo. "Sobre el escritorio emilianense en los siglos X y XI." *Boletín de la Real Academia de la Historia*, CXLIII (1958), 7-19.

The scribe of the *Nota* also wrote parts of the Roda Codex of the San Millán scriptorium. A scrutiny of the latter MS. provides verification that he was active between 1035 and 1086, and, if the variations in his hand can be ascribed to chronological development, the *Nota* may well be contemporary with *O*. rev: Colombás, *RHE*, LV (1960), 701.

489   Aebischer, Paul. "Un Echo norrois d'un détail curieux fourni par la *Nota Emilianense.*" *CN*, XXVIII (1968), 5-15.

The *neptis* of the *Nota* are not "nephews" but "grandsons", and result from an attempt to translate the Latin *aulici*, or some such word. rev: Di Stefano, *SF*, XIV (1970), 318.

490   Richthofen, Erich von. "Problemas rolandinos, almerienses y cidianos." *AEM*, V (1968), 437-44. Repr. in *Tradicionalismo épico-novelesco*, Barcelona: Editorial Planeta, 1972. Pp. 11-22.

The "paragogic -e" of certain names in the *Nota* does not prove the existence of a Spanish *CR* predating *O*.

491   Horrent, Jacques. "Ganelon, le conseil des barons, et la *Nota Emilianense.*" *Mélanges Le Gentil*, pp. 367-75.

Ch's council is unhistorical and exists in the *R* tradition only as a pretext for presenting the conflict between Ganelon and R. Both the council and the fact that R commands the rearguard must derive from a poetic source of the *Nota*.

492   ——. "Les Noms *Rodlane* et *Bertlane* dans la *Nota Emilianense.*" *Hommage à Maurice Delbouille*, pp. 231-49.

See also 541, 542, 559.

ONOMASTICS

Onomastic studies touching upon the *CR* concern mainly either the origins of proper names (R, Oliver, Durendal) or the occurrence, in documents of the eleventh and twelfth centuries, of the names R and Oliver. Mentions of the two names in the same document are especially significant when it can be shown that they belong to brothers, evidence that the legend of R and Oliver was known at the time. Pio Rajna was the first to study this question (*Romania*, XVIII [1889], 1-69), but the full significance of the phenomenon was not realized until it was taken up by Ferdinand Lot (524).

The binomial Roland-Oliver.

493   Lejeune, Rita. "La Naissance du couple littéraire 'R et Olivier'." *Mélanges Henri Grégoire*, vol. II. *Annuaire de l'Institut de Philologie et d'Histoire Orientales et Slaves*, X (1950), 371-401.

The five examples of the pair R-Oliver found up to this date in eleventh-

c. documents all come from the Midi and are evidence that the R legend or poem on which they are based is of Southern French origin. Documentation based on the examination of 130 cartularies.

494   Aebischer, Paul. "Les Trois plus Anciennes Mentions du couple 'R-Olivier'." *RBPH*, XXX (1952), 657-75.

The oldest mentions are those of Saint-Aubin d'Angers (1082-1106) and Saint-Pé de Générès (1096).

495   McMillan, Duncan. "Du nouveau sur la *CR*?" *MLR*, XLVII (1952), 334-9.

The act of donation from Saint-Victor de Marseille which mentions R and Oliver has been shown to be a forgery dating from after 1119 (and probably after 1150), on the basis of internal evidence presented by M. E.H. Duprat ("Marseille et la *CR*", *Vérité* [a Marseilles weekly], no. 106, October 11, 1956).

496   Aebischer, Paul. "Un Cas du couple R-Olivier dans une charte de San Cugat del Vallés." *BRABLB*, XXV (1953), 165-70.

Brothers *Olivarius* (a priest) and *Rodlandus*, sons of an *Oliverius*, would have been born around 1110.

497   ——. "A propos de deux ou trois nouveaux cas italiens du couple R et Olivier." *CN*, XV (1955), 223-37.

A document from Venice, dated 1183, mentions brothers named Rolandus and Oliverius; a forged document from Arezzo, probably from the late twelfth c., mentions Turpin, R, and Oliver. The order Oliver-R, found in eleventh-c. documents, may derive from the popularity of an early version of *Girart de Vienne*, a poem in which R plays the subsidiary role.

498   ——. "L'Entrée de R et d'Olivier dans le vocabulaire onomastique de la Marca Hispanica d'après le *Liber Feudorum Maior* et d'autres recueils de chartes catalanes et françaises." *Estudis Romànics*, V (1955-6), 55-76.

Olivarius rivals the older form Oliba from around 1053 in Catalonia; the name R entered at around the same time. The charter of Brioude (first third of the eleventh c.), while a forgery, may not be a complete falsification. R and Oliver do not represent the *topos fortitudo-sapientia.*

499   Scalia, Giuseppe. "*Oliverius* e *Rolandus* nel *Liber Maiorichinus*." *SMV*, IV (1956), 285-301.

An example of the binomial dating from around 1135 probably results from the medieval author's desire to evoke the companionship of R and Oliver.

500   Rosellini, Aldo. "*Onomastica rolandiana*: Un nuovo caso

italiano del binomio Orlando e Oliviero." *CN*, XVIII (1958), 53-8.

Orlando and *Oliverio*, brothers in a document from Ferrara dated 1176. Orlando is the elder. rev: De Cesare, *SF*, III (1959), 115.

501 Aebischer, Paul. *"Onomastica rolandiana*: Un nouveau cas génois du couple R et Olivier." *CN*, XVIII (1958), 59-60.

Two charters from Genoa, dated 1150, mention the brothers *Rollandus* and *Oliverius*. rev: De Cesare, *SF*, III (1959), 115.

502 Vajay, Szabolcs de. "Rayonnement de la *CR*: Le couple anthroponyme 'R et Olivier' en Hongrie médiévale." *MA*, LXVIII (1962), 321-9.

The Ratot family, whose ancestors Oliverius and Ratold came to Hungary in 1097 from Sicily, claimed descent from R.

503 Van Emden, Wolfgang G. *"Rolandiana et Oliveriana*: Faits et hypothèses." *Romania*, XCII (1971), 507-31.

Neither the order of names Oliver-R nor the *Karlamagnús saga* necessarily attests *Girart de Vienne* antedating *O*, contrary to the hypotheses of Paul Aebischer. rev: Stramignoni, *SF*, XVII (1974), 322.

503A Aebischer, Paul. *"Oliveriana et Rolandiana*: Sur le résumé du *Girart de Viane* conservé par la première branche de la *Karlamagnús saga*. Une ultime mise au point." *RBPH*, LI (1973), 517-33.

Reaffirms the existence of an early *Girart de Vienne* on the basis of the *Karlamagnús saga*, against Van Emden's objections (503).

See also 487, 529, 541, 542, 559, 568.

Other onomastic studies.

504 Coll i Alentorn, Miquel. "La introducció de les llegendes èpiques franceses a Catalunya." *Coloquios de Roncesvalles*, pp. 133-50.

Review of the evidence for knowledge of the French epic in Catalonia, based mostly on the occurrence of proper names. The cycle of Ch was known from around 1030.

505 Rosellini, Aldo. "Onomastica epica francese in Italia nel medioevo." *Romania*, LXXIX (1958), 253-67.

Sceptical reconsideration of Pio Rajna's conclusions on names as evidence for the diffusion of *chansons de geste* in Italy.

506 Capitani, Liana. "Da Hrodland a Orlando." *SMV*, XI (1963), 69-73.

On the evolution in the form of R's name.

507 Camproux, Charles. "A propos du nom de R." *RIO*, XVI (1964), 63-6.

The root *hroth-, hrod-*, "glory, victory", may have led the bilingual population of early medieval France to attach to R's name the contrasting figure of Oliver, whose name connotes wisdom and peace.

508 Louis, René. "De Livier à Olivier." *Mélanges Delbouille*, vol. II, pp. 447-76.

Suggests the working hypothesis that Oliver may derive from St Livier of Metz.

509 Richthofen, Erich von. "Considérations complémentaires sur les légendes épiques et les romans courtois." *Mélanges Delbouille*, vol. II, pp. 581-96. Pp. 591-6 revised and tr. as "¿Hacia una nueva cronología?" *Nuevos estudios*, pp. 129-35.

Nobles is Coimbra. Turpin, archbishop of Rheims, is a transformation of Bernard of Toledo, through the fusion of the elements of an abbreviation: "[en *To*ledo] *prim*as uenerandus . . . *Raym*undus *episcopus*." Other identifications of a similarly fantastic nature. rev: D'Heur, *MR*, XX (1970), 117-18.

510 Broéns, Maurice. "Les Noms propres wisigoths dans la *CR*." *BRABLB*, XXXI (1965-6), 65-71.

Visigothic roots can be seen behind many Saracen names.

511 Radojičić, Djordje Sp. "Un Poème épique yougoslave du XIe siècle: Les *Gesta* ou exploits de Vladimir, prince de Dioclée." *Byzantion*, XXXV (1965), 528-35.

Flurit (v. 3211) would derive from the epithet of Vladimir, "le Bienheureux", OFr *flurit*, symbolizing the happiness of paradise.

512 Ruggieri, Ruggero M. "Expressivité et polymorphisme dans l'onomastique de l'ancienne littérature chevaleresque française et italienne." *MA*, LXXI (1965), 275-88.

Phonomorphological and semantic metamorphoses in the names of Saracen heroes and gods, and in those of Alda and Olimpia.

513 Schmittlein, Raymond. "Le Nom d'Olivier." *RIO*, XVIII (1966), 301-3.

The name derives from the Germanic Altwar or Alitgar.

514 Aebischer, Paul. "La Véritable Identité d'Antoine, duc d'Avignon et père d'Aye d'Avignon." *MR*, XVIII (1968), 147-55.

Material on the Austorje de Valence of v. 1625.

515 Pirot, François. "Olivier de Lausanne et Olivier de Verdu(n): Sur les traces d'une épopée occitane?" *Mélanges Lejeune*, vol. I, pp. 247-65.

Oliver of Verdu(n) is not the companion of R, but a separate hero who must have been the subject of poems in the *langue d'oc.*

516 Rohlfs, Gerhard. " 'Ci conte de Durendal l'espee'." *Mélanges Lejeune*, vol. II, pp. 859-69. A reworking of "Was bedeutet der Schwertname Durendal?" *Archiv*, CLXIX (1936), 57-64.

The original form was *Durendart*, with the meaning *"dur-end-art"*, "il brûle fort dehors", "une forte ou mauvaise flamme en sort".

517 Aebischer, Paul. "L'Etat actuel des recherches relatives aux origines de l'anthroponyme Olivier." *Mélanges Frappier*, vol. I, pp. 17-34.

The name has no symbolic significance in the *CR*, despite Spitzer's claim. The name's origin is still in doubt.

518 ——."Notule rolandienne: Les personnages d'Astor et de Gaifier dans la laisse LXIV du *R* d'Oxford." *MA*, LXXVI (1970), 427-43.

O is incomplete in this laisse and in laisse CLXII. Astor and Austorge (v. 1625) are both vernacular forms of Eustorgius, itself of Greek origin. rev: Baldinger, *ZRP*, LXXXVII (1971), 652; Di Stefano, *SF*, XV (1971), 230.

519 Galmés de Fuentes, Álvaro. " 'Les nums d'Almace et cels de Durendal' (*CR*, v. 2143): Probable origen árabe del nombre de las dos famosas espadas." *Studia hispanica in honorem R. Lapesa.* Vol. I. Madrid: Gredos and Cátedra-Seminario Menéndez Pidal, 1972. Pp. 228-41.

Almace would come from *almãs*, "diamond", and Durendal from *du l-'andar*, "of brilliant quality, shining". The latter derivation would be consonant with vv. 2316-17.

ORIGINS, GENESIS, AND SOURCES

Since the *CR* is the oldest complete French epic now extant, the question of its origins cannot be separated from that of the rise of the *chanson de geste* as a whole. Theories are as numerous as the authors writing on the problem, but several more or less distinct tendencies can be discerned. Paradoxically, many of the more recent theoreticians have returned to a position close to that of Gaston Paris and other nineteenth-c. figures, who posited a continuous tradition of unrecorded songs going back to the time of Charlemagne or even to the event itself. In this group, called by Menéndez Pidal "traditionalists", there is, however, a split between those for whom the oral tradition is essentially based upon transmission through memory and those who see it as a less conservative process of improvisational composition. Nevertheless Bédier's position that the genre is the creation of great individuals, writing in substantially the same way as modern authors, is still very much alive, and its defenders, although generally modifying their position from Bédier's to take account of new factual material (in particular the *Nota Emilianense*),lean toward clerical or even classical influence to explain the *CR*'s coherence. Thus the matter of origins is often confounded with source studies, and clerical or other literary antecedents are taken as signs in favor of *bédiériste* notions. Of course many scholars —perhaps the majority— have taken positions between the two extremes, or have spoken for the idea that the genesis of each *chanson de geste* is to be explained as a phenomenon unto itself.

520   Paris, Gaston. *Histoire poétique de Ch.* Paris: Franck, 1865. Second edition, 1905.

What was, until Bédier's *Légendes épiques*, the most influential work on French epic origins. A continuous tradition of *cantilenae* links the epic with the historical event upon which it is based. The earliest *chansons de geste* begin to take shape toward the middle of the tenth c.

521   Rajna, Pio. *Le origini dell' epopea francese.* Florence: Sansoni, 1884. Repr. 1956.

Germanic origins.

522   Bédier, Joseph. *Les Légendes épiques: Recherches sur la formation des chansons de geste.* 4 vols. Paris: Champion, 1908-13. Second ed.: 1914-21. Third ed.: 1926-9.

A complete re-examination of the question of epic origins which brought its author a just fame both in erudite circles and among the cultivated French public. The *chanson de geste*, born in the eleventh c., is the collaborative creation of *jongleurs* and monks who wished to attract travelers to their churches and monasteries, which dotted the great pilgrimage routes and principally those leading to Rome and Santiago de Compostela. "Au commencement était la route." Although this theory, itself a reaction against the ideas of Gaston Paris, has passed through the stage of orthodoxy only to come itself under a barrage of criticism during the last several decades, Bédier's book still contains a wealth of information and astute historical criticism. The *CR* is treated in vol. III, pp. 183-453. After surveying the various theories, Bédier links the poem with a series of toponyms found along the section of the pilgrimage route to Santiago leading from Bordeaux to Pamplona. The poem was written in the year 1100 at the earliest, by a single poet who based himself on local legends. The historical element is derived from a single page of Einhard's *Vita Karoli*. After a brilliant literary analysis, "L'unité du poème: *Turoldus vindicatus*," Bédier maintains that such a well-constructed work of art can only be the creation of an individual poet of genius. For an evaluation of what remains valid in Bédier's theory, see 27. See also 577.

523   Boissonnade, Prosper. *Du nouveau sur la CR: La genèse historique, le cadre géographique, le milieu, les personnages, la date et l'auteur du poème*. Paris: Champion, 1923.

Stresses the role of the eleventh-c. crusades into Spain, attempting to identify the place-names with Spanish toponyms.

524   Lot, Ferdinand. "Etudes sur les légendes épiques françaises, V: la *CR*. A propos d'un livre récent." *Romania*, LIV (1928), 357-80. Repr. in *Etudes sur les légendes épiques françaises*. Edited by Robert Bossuat. Paris: Champion, 1958. Pp. 260-79.

Occasioned by Boissonnade's book. The *CR* shows no trace of clerical origin. The tradition according to which it was sung at the Battle of Hastings is trustworthy. Lot reveals documentation proving the existence of brothers named R and Oliver in 1096, arguing that the poem was well known before that date. The "France" of vv. 1428-9 conforms to the tenth-c. *Francia* and is an archaism which also militates in favor of an ancient R tradition. This article gave major impetus to the reaction against Bédier's theory.

525   Fawtier, Robert. *La CR: Etude historique*. Paris: Boccard, 1933.

On the basis of eye-witness accounts of the historical Battle of Roncevaux, poets composed the first ballads about R which developed into a longer poem sometime during the tenth c. Certain scenes in *O* go back to the ballad materials and style. R.F.'s thesis that the defeat of Ch's rearguard was a major disaster is now accepted by many.

526   Pauphilet, Albert. "Sur la *CR*." *Romania*, LIX (1933), 161-8.

"Au commencement était le poète."

527   Siciliano, Italo. *Le origini delle canzoni di gesta: Teorie e discussioni*. (Collana Ca' Foscari, Sezione Lingue e Letterature Straniere, Venezia) Padua: Dottore Antonio Milani,

1940. *Les Origines des chansons de geste: Théories et discussions.* Translated by P. Antonetti. Paris: A. et J. Picard, 1951.

A complete review of the question, concluding in Bédier's favor.

528   Li Gotti, Ettore. *La CR e i Normanni.* Florence: Sansoni, 1949.

The *CR* has Norman origins, Turoldus being Turoldus of Peterborough (also called Turoldus of Fécamp), the author rather than the scribe. The *geste* of v. 4002 is his source.

529   Delbouille, Maurice. *Sur la genèse de la CR: Travaux récents, propositions nouvelles. Essai critique.* (Académie Royale de Langue et de Littérature Françaises de Belgique) Brussels: Palais des Académies, 1954.

A work occasioned by Jules Horrent's book (609), which was written as a thesis under M.D.'s direction. Discrepancies between *O* and other versions are imputed to scribal negligence rather than to the will of a *remanieur*. A short *CR* was written in Anjou toward the beginning of the eleventh c. The Episode of Baligant is not a late addition. Turoldus, who lived in the region between Paris and Orleans, wrote the poem which we have in *O*, and was versed in both Latin and vernacular stylistic traditions. M.D. devotes considerable discussion to the anthroponyms R and Oliver, and opposes both Rita Lejeune's hypothesis of a Southern French origin and André Burger's assumption of a Latin source for *O*.

530   Lejeune, Rita. "Actualité de la *CR*." *NC*, VII (1955), 207-27.

The pair of names R-Oliver spread from southern France toward the north. Formulaic composition of the *chanson de geste* indicates oral provenience. An abundance of variants is caused by the multitude of improvising *jongleurs*. rev: Roques, *Romania*, LXXVIII (1957), 283.

531   Le Gentil, Pierre. "A propos de l'origine des chansons de geste: Le problème de l'auteur." *Coloquios de Roncesvalles*, pp. 113-21.

The author of the *CR*, neither a cleric nor a *jongleur* but partaking of the art of both, was an individual artist composing on the basis of an oral tradition.

532   Louis, René. "L'Epopée française est carolingienne." *Coloquios de Roncesvalles*, pp. 327-460.

A global treatment of the historical element in the *chanson de geste*. The transmission of R's name from the eighth-c. event to the poem can be explained only by an orally-transmitted poetic tradition. Local legends of Blaye or Roncevaux played no part in the genesis of the *CR*.

533   Menéndez Pidal, Ramón. "La *CR* desde el punto de vista del tradicionalismo." *Coloquios de Roncesvalles*, pp. 15-37.

A succinct statement of the author's views on the nature of the *chanson de geste* and the role of variants in its creation. See 541 and 542.

534   Viscardi, Antonio. "Credo quia absurdum." *FR*, III (1956), 342-70.

Medieval French epic is neither historical nor of popular origin; before the *CR* was nothing.

535   ——."In principio era il poeta." *Annali della Facoltà di Filosofia e Lettere dell'Università Statale di Milano*, IX (1956), 31-56.

The *CR* precedes the medieval French epic, rather than deriving from an earlier tradition. rev: Lausberg, *Archiv*, CXCIV (1958), 360-1.

536   Aebischer, Paul. "*Raimbaud et Hamon*: Une source perdue de la *CR*." *MA*, LXIII (1957), 23-54. Repr. in *Rolandiana et Oliveriana*, pp. 35-55.

Chapters 18 and 28-32 of the First Branch of the *Karlamagnús saga* are the résumé of a lost *chanson de geste, Raimbaud et Hamon*, which predates *O*.

537   Minis, Cola. "Über Rolands Horn, Burgers *Passio Rothlandi,* und Konrads *Roland*." *Mélanges Frank*, pp. 439-53.

Supports André Burger's hypothesis (*Romania*, LXX [1949], 433-73) of a Latin *Passio* prior to *O*. rev: Muraille, *CCM*, II (1959), 479.

538   Riquer, Martín de. "Respuesta a Antonio Viscardi." *FR*, IV (1957), 355-61.

Criticizes Viscardi's faith in concepts such as the philosophy of art, rejecting the notion that before the *CR* there was nothing.

539   Battaglia, Salvatore. "Il medioevo dei giullari e la *CR*." *FR*, V (1958), 225-46. Repr. as "La trasmissione giullaresca." *La coscienza letteraria*, pp. 63-89.

Medieval epic is of oral formation, and was transmitted by *jongleurs* whose culture had its own forms, models, and techniques. The *CR* was something of an exception, since, although it is a product of *jongleresque* culture, it was elaborated by a man of genius.

540   Delbouille, Maurice. "Les Chansons de geste et le livre: Travaux récents." *La Technique littéraire*, pp. 295-407.

There is no difference in MS. transmission between the *chanson de geste* and other medieval genres. The *trouvère-poète* is responsible for creation, the *jongleur-exécutant* for performance.

541 Menéndez Pidal, Ramón. *La CR y el neotradicionalismo: Orígenes de la épica románica.* Madrid: Espasa-Calpe, 1959.
One of the notable achievements of *R* scholarship. The author's thesis is that a continuous poetic tradition links the extant texts to the historical event. In the early stages of this tradition, born of a song created to inform the public of the disaster (a *canto noticiero*), the legend lived in a latent state, that is in poems unrecorded by the clergy, which was not interested in secular literature. The *CR* was a poem in continuous transformation, undergoing minute but constant changes effected by a legion of poets who passed it on in oral tradition in order to preserve the memory of great historical figures. "En el principio era la historia." The *chanson de geste* as a whole is a genre whose life is inseparable from its transformations ("una poesía que vive en variantes y en refundiciones"). Their complexity explains why it is impossible to construct a coherent stemma of MS. filiation for the *CR*. R.M.P. characterizes Bédier's *Turoldus vindicatus* (522) as *Turoldus deplumatus*. *O* is a good version, but it is not *précellent*, being in places inferior to others and notably to *V4*. The introductory chapter surveys theories on the origin and nature of the *CR*. An appendix contains the text of important Latin and Arabic sources. rev: Lecoy, *Romania*, LXXX (1959), 419-23; Levy, *Books Abroad*, XXXIII (1959), 414-15; Garciasol, *CHA*, XXXVIII (1959), 253-8; Bataillon, *CRAIBL*, 1959, pp. 129-30; Soria, *Arbor*, XLIII bis (1959), 451-8; Sanchis Guarner, *Papeles de Son Armadans*, XIII (1959), 329-40; Benavides Lillo, *Anales de la Univ de Chile*, CXVIII (1960), 169-70; Sholod, *RR*, LI (1960), 211-15; Favati, *SF*, IV (1960), 95-9; Aebischer, *ZRP*, LXXVI (1960), 29-44; Heger, *RJ*, XI (1960), 256-62; Sandmann, *GRM*, X (1960), 361-9; Marx, *EC*, IX (1960-1), 605-6; Bourciez, *RLR*, LXXIV (1960-1), 269-73; Condeescu, *Rev. de Filologie Romanică și Germanică*, V (1961), 87-95; Beau, *Revista Portuguesa de Filologia*, XI (1961), 467-70; Bertrand, *Cuadernos de Historia de España*, XXXIII-XXXIV (1961), 373-6.

542 ——. *La CR et la tradition épique des Francs.* Translation of the Spanish edition by Irénée-Marcel Cluzel, with revision carried out by the author with the collaboration of René Louis. Paris: A. et J. Picard, 1960.
rev: Grégoire, *Flambeau*, XLIII (1960), 645-9; Favati, *SF*, V (1961), 316; Thérive, *Table Ronde*, no. 157 (February 1961), 186-90; Pognon, *Revue de Paris*, LXVIII, no. 12 (December 1961), 143-8; also *NC*, X-XII (1958-62), 199-205; Sandmann, *GRM*, XII (1962), 104-6; Le Gentil, *CCM*, V (1962), 323-33; Payen, *MA*, LXVIII (1962), 395-405; Wilsdorf, *MA*, LXVIII (1962), 405-17; Viscardi, *Fiera Letteraria*, VIII (1962), 143-92; also in *Romania: Scritti offerti a F. Piccolo* (Naples: Armanni, 1962), pp. 527-34; Walpole, *Speculum*, XXXVIII (1963), 373-82; Sallefranque, *Cahiers du Sud*, L (1963), 216-26; Puppo, LI, XVI (1964), 80-5.

See also 19-26, 73, 121, 546, 552, 554, 559, 560, 567.

543   Vantuch, Anton. "Poeta Saxo a starofrancúzske epické
        spevy [The Saxon Poet and French epic songs]." *Litteraria:*
        Stúdie a Dokumenty, II (1959), 286-353. In Slovak, with
        French résumé pp. 342-53.

        The Saxon Poet's *vulgaria carmina* are French rather than Germanic, as
        the latter would have been called *barbara carmina*. See Rita Lejeune's
        comment (548).

544   De Vries, Jan. *Heldenlied en heldensage*. Utrecht and
        Antwerp: Uitgeverij Het Spectrum, Aula-goeken, 1959.
        Heldenlied und Heldensage. (Sammlung Dalp, LXXVIII)
        Berne: Francke Verlag, 1961.
        Heroic Song and Heroic Legend. Translated by B. J. Timmer.
        (Oxford Paperbacks, LXIX) London: Oxford Univ. Press,
        1963.

        CR: pp. 22-35 of the English tr. The Oxford poet did have pre-
        decessors going back before the year 1000, authors of short epic songs
        in the vernacular. But the example of a clerical, Latin epic was neces-
        sary to crystallize these songs into the form of a full-length epic. A
        Latin precursor to *O* is thus assumed. rev: Le Roux, *Ogam*, XII (1960),
        250-1; Lukman, *CCM*, VII (1964), 359-63.

545   Aebischer, Paul. "La *CR* dans le 'désert littéraire' du XIe
        siècle." *RBPH*, XXXVIII (1960), 718-49. Repr. in
        Rolandiana et Oliveriana, pp. 56-80.

        The eleventh-c. French epic was already a complex and rich genre. rev:
        Favati, *SF*, V (1961), 315-16; Masai, *Scriptorium*, XV (1961), 127.

546   Burger, André. "La Question rolandienne: Faits et
        hypothèses." *CCM*, IV (1961), 121.

        Criticizes the neotraditionalist interpretation of texts and documents,
        maintaining that the R legend cannot be proven to have existed before
        the eleventh c.

547   Hall, Robert A., Jr. "On Individual Authorship in the *R*."
        Symposium, XV (1961), 297-302.

        Varying systems of assonance lead to the conclusion of multiple author-
        ship.

548   Lejeune, Rita. "Le Poète Saxon et les chants épiques
        français." *MA*, LXVII (1961), 137-47.

        Commentary on Vantuch's article (543), with bibliographical additions.

549   ——. "Quelques réflexions sur la genèse de la *CR*." *Gai Saber*,
        CCC (1961), 1-16.

        Accepts the neotraditionalist point of view, while regarding Turoldus as a poet of genius.

550   Mandach, André de. *Naissance et développement de la
chanson de geste en Europe:* Vol. I. *La geste de Ch et de R.*
Vol. II. *Chronique de Turpin, texte anglo-norman inédit de
Willem de Briane.* (PRF, LXIX and LXXVII) Geneva: Droz,
1961-3.

A general theory on the development of the genre. A heroic climate
generates the epic cycle after a period of incubation. The force of Ch's
myth derives from an association with Alfonso VI of Castile, the
conqueror of Toledo, symbol of both imperial aspirations and the
Crusade. The Carolingian tradition has two major branches: the Turpin-
ian and the Turoldian. Turoldus' poem is only one stage, preceding the
introduction of the Episode of Baligant, but Turoldus was an author-
reworker of great talent. rev: Jones, *Speculum*, XXXVII (1962), 634-7;
Vàrvaro, *SF*, VI (1962), 521-3; Ruggieri, *SM*, III (1962), 632-7; J.
Bourciez, *RLR*, LXXV (1962-3), 135-7; Adler, *Archiv*, CXCIX (1962-
3), 425-6; Segre, *ZRP*, LXXIX (1963), 437-45; Bernhard, *Neue Zürcher
Zeitung*, May 10, 1963, Morgenausgabe, no. 1881; Thorpe, *Scriptorium*,
XVII (1963), 383-4; Payen, *RPh*, XVII (1963-4), 481-5; Bahner,
Deutsche Literaturzeitung, LXXXV (1965), 209-11; Walpole, *MLR*, LX
(1965),613-18; Ziltener, *ZRP*, LXXXIII (1967), 119-24.

551   Le Gentil, Pierre. "Les Chansons de geste et le problème de
la création littéraire au moyen âge: 'Remaniement' et
'mutation brusque'." *Mélanges offerts à Marcel Bataillon par
les hispanistes français.* Edited by Maxime Chevalier, Robert
Picard, and Noël Salomon. Bordeaux: Féret et Fils, 1962.
BH, LXIV *bis* (1962), 490-7.

Like a master modeler retouching a statue whose clay is still soft but
whose primary form has been set by lesser men, the *remanieur de génie*
brings about a *mutation brusque* in the poetic tradition. The ideas of
neotraditionalists and individualists can be reconciled through this conception of the poet responsible for *O*'s greatness.

552   Whitehead, Frederick. "Menéndez Pidal and the *CR*." *BHS*,
XXXIX (1962), 31-3.

Affirms the individualist thesis, with emphasis on the importance of Ch
as a political symbol.

553   Heisig, Paul. "Turoldus und Vergil." *GRM*, XIII (1963),
204-6.

The disruption of nature in anticipation of R's death is inspired by
scenes from Virgil's *Eclogues* and *Georgics*. rev: De Cesare, *SF*, VIII
(1964), 124.

554   Robson, Charles Alan. "Une *CR* gasconne?" *BRABLB*,

XXXI (1965-6), 251-63.

O is seen, on the basis of assonantal types, to result from the amalgamation of previous versions, one of which was a Gascon text.

555 Aebischer, Paul. "Trois personnages en quête d'auteur: R, Olivier, Aude. Contribution à la génétique de la CR." *Festschrift Walter Baetke: Dargebracht zu seinem 80. Geburtstag am 28. März 1964.* Edited by Kurt Rudolph, Rolf Heller, and Ernest Walter. Weimar: Böhlau, 1966. Pp. 17-45. Repr. in *Rolandiana et Oliveriana*, pp. 141-73.

The character Oliver was created by the author of an early *Girart de Vienne* as a counterbalance to R, both being nephews of the poem's protagonists.

556 Monteverdi, Angelo. "A proposito della *CR*." *Studi Siciliano*, pp. 861-2.

Nothing is known of the *CR*'s antecedents, nor of the methods of the first *R* poet.

557 Sholod, Barton. *Ch in Spain: The Cultural Legacy of Roncesvalles.* Geneva: Droz, 1966.

A largely derivative work of synthesis treating Ch's Sin, the development of the R legend in oral tradition, the importance of Ch's historical defeat in Spain, the interplay between French and Spanish culture and politics, the pilgrimage to Santiago, the *Pseudo-Turpin Chronicle*, the genesis of the *CR*, and the survival of Carolingian legends in Spanish folklore: rev: Williamson, *SF*, XII (1968), 326-7; Mandach, *BHR*, XXXI (1969), 405-7.

558 Duggan, Joseph J. "Virgilian Inspiration in the *Roman d'Enéas* and the *CR*." *Medieval Epic to the Epic Theater of Brecht.* Edited by Rosario P. Armato and John M. Spalek. (Univ. of Southern California Studies in Comparative Literature, I) Los Angeles: Univ. of Southern California Press, 1968. Pp. 9-23.

Lack of Virgilian influence on the *CR* is shown through an analysis of thematic and stylistic features common to the *Aeneid* and the *Roman d'Enéas*, but absent from the *CR*.

559 Siciliano, Italo. *Les Chansons de geste et l'épopée: Mythes, histoire, poèmes.* (Biblioteca di Studi Francesi, III) Turin: Società Editrice Internazionale, 1968. Also Paris: A. et J. Picard, 1970.

A criticism, at times vituperative, of the neotraditionalist position. The beginning and the end of all poetic creation is the individual. The *chanson de geste* cannot be shown to have existed before the eleventh c., and was motivated by sentiments which are typical not of a popular milieu but of the knightly caste. "Au commencement du genre était la caste." "Collective composition" is a myth. The author characterizes his work as "un gros livre pour annoncer qu'il n'y a rien de nouveau" since his previous book on epic origins (527)! A concluding section contains an interpretive reading of the *CR* and three other epics. rev: Di Stefano, *SF*, XIII (1969), 521-2; Segre, *LI*, XXI (1969), 494-8; Etiemble, *Le Monde*, October 11, 1969; Jodogne, *SF*, XIV (1970), 107-12; *TLS*, September 18, 1970, 1032; Kennedy, *MLR*, LXV (1970), 895-6; Guiette, *RBPH*, XLVIII (1970), 60-1; Rickard, *MAe*, XXXIX (1970), 182-6; Cordie, *Paideia*, XXV (1970), 241-2; Calin, *RR*, LXII (1971), 133-4; Nichols, *Comparative Literature*, XXIII (1971), 262-4; McMillan, *FS*, XXVI (1972), 179-80; Delbouille, *CCM*, XV (1972), 205-21; Horrent, *MA*, LXXIX (1973), 269-83.

560   Aebischer, Paul. "Le Concept d'*état latent* dans la préhistoire des chansons de geste." *RBPH*, XLVII (1969), 789-839.

Admits the validity of Menéndez Pidal's concept, here defined as a state of gestation between the historical event and the poetic creation, for the *CR*, among other *chansons de geste*. A major statement on the relation between history and the epic. rev: Baldinger, *ZRP*, LXXXVI (1970), 677.

561   Vantuch, Anton. "Réflexions sur la légende de Ch aux IXe-Xe siècles." *Mélanges Lejeune*, vol. II, pp. 919-28.

A non-clerical legend of Ch did exist at the time, as proven by the Saxon Poet. rev: Joset, *MA*, LXXVI (1970), 536.

562   McMillan, Duncan. "*Dispendium habuit grande*: Notule rolandienne." *Mélanges Frappier*, vol. II, pp. 697-700.

This phrase from the *Annales Sangallenses Baluzii* can be explained by a supposed visit of Ch to St-Gall.

563   Viscardi, Antonio. "Origini giullaresche o troveriche delle canzone di gesta?" *Rendiconti dell'Istituto Lombardo di Scienze e Lettere, Milano, Classe di Lettere e Scienze Morali e Storiche*, CIV (1970), 61-78.

Jongleurs are incapable of creating a work of the *CR*'s quality. Critique of Battaglia (539).

564   Siciliano, Italo. "Il problema della formazione dell'epopea carolingia." *La poesia epica*, pp. 263-75.

The *chanson de geste* is a poetic phenomenon which did not exist before the synthesis of all of its elements was carried out in the mind and artistry of one poet.

565   Ohly, Friedrich. "Zu den Ursprüngen der *CR*." *Medievalia*

Litteraria: Festschrift für Helmut de Boor zum 80. Geburts-tag. Edited by Ursula Hennig and Herbert Kolb. Munich: Beck, 1971. Pp. 135-53.

A troop of Franks under Duke Arnebert was ambushed in the Soule Valley of the Pyrenees near Roncevaux in 636 or 637. Memories of this event, and also of an incident in the life of St Amandus, converter of the Basques, may have given rise to a legend which was later fused with the defeat of Ch's rearguard to form the *CR*.

566   Richthofen, Erich von. "Une Critique textuelle concernant Roncevaux, les Infants de Lara et le Cid dans les Chroniques de Castille." *BBSR*, VI (1971), 150-1. Résumé. To appear in the proceedings of the Oxford Congress of the Société Rencesvals.

The account of Roncevaux found in the *Primera crónica general* is based on Einhard, but shows the influence of epic poetry.

567   Viscardi, Antonio. "La tradizione storiografica dei secoli VIII-X relativa alla campagna iberica del 778 dà testimonianza dell'*histoire chantée*?" *Studi di filologia romanza offerti a Silvio Pellegrini.* Padua: Liviana Editrice, 1971. Pp. 667-74.

Defends Pellegrini against a criticism of Rita Lejeune [*CCM*, IV (1968), 625-8], and denies that Carolingian historiography supports the idea of *histoire chantée*.

568   Aebischer, Paul. *Préhistoire et protohistoire du R d'Oxford.* (Bibliotheca Romanica, Series Prima, Manualia et Commentationes, XII) Berne: Francke Verlag, 1972.

A major study in which P.A. places himself among the individualists as far as artistic creation is concerned, although he affirms the existence of a rich epic tradition in the eleventh c. Much of the material is found in the author's previous studies on the historical event, onomastics, the original title, the final lines, the Episode of Baligant, and the *chansons de geste* preceding *O* whose existence is reflected in the First Branch of the *Karlamagnús saga*. This book thus represents a synthesis of P.A.'s contributions to R studies. rev: Di Stefano, *SF*, XVII (1973), 109; Drzewicka, *Kwartalnik Neofilologiczny*, XX (1973), 441-4; Ross, *MAe*, XLIII (1974), 159; Verhuyck, *Neophilologus*, LVIII (1974), 92-3.

569   Richthofen, Erich von. "Conjeturas sobre un primitivo *Cid* y *Roland* ('tradicionalismo', 'individualismo' y positivismo)." *Tradicionalismo épico-novelesco.* Barcelona: Planeta, 1972. Pp. 23-36. Originally printed in *Prohemio*, I (1970), 414-24.

The terms "traditionalism" and "individualism" should be done away with as they apply to epic studies, perhaps in favor of a term such as "positivism".

570   Horrent, Jacques. "L'*Historia silense* ou *seminense*." *MR*,
       XXIII (1973), nos 2-4, and XXIV (1974), nos 1-2, pp. 135-
       50.

       The chronicle attacks the claims of Carolingian historiography and its
       author did not have the *CR* in mind. See also 611.

See also 28, 29, 36, 214, 333, 344, 360, 376, 384, 393, 397, 409,
410.

RELATION TO ELEVENTH AND TWELFTH-CENTURY HISTORY

The Oxford *CR* also reflects the history and customs of the time at
which it was first composed, that is to say a period roughly contemporary with the First Crusade.

571   Richthofen, Erich von. "Interpretaciones histórico-legenda-
       rias en la épica medieval." *Arbor*, XXX (1955), 177-96.
       Repr. in *Nuevos estudios*, pp. 9-29.

       The *CR* fuses elements from eleventh-c. Spanish history with Carolingian
       legends.

572   Klein, Hans-Wilhelm. "Der Kreuzzugsgedanke im *Rolandslied*
       und die neuere Rolandsforschung." *Die Neueren Sprachen*,
       Neue Folge, V (1956), 265-85.

       The *CR* shows influences of the crusading period.

573   Frappier, Jean. "Réflexions sur les rapports des chansons de
       geste et de l'histoire." *ZRP*, LXXIII (1957), 1-19.

       An important study. Among other matters, some aspects of the *CR* are
       treated: the Saracen gods, the peoples named in Baligant's 30 *échelles*,
       the poem's versification and art. These are seen as the result of a long
       development prior to the *CR*'s composition. rev: De Cesare, *SF*, II
       (1958), 112; Goosse, *LR*, XII (1958), 94; Cézard, *Romania*, LXXIX
       (1958), 281-2.

574   Douglas, David C. "The *Song of Roland* and the Norman
       Conquest of England." *FS*, XIV (1960), 99-116.

       Ch's supposed conquest of England (vv. 373-4, 2331-2) may have been
       inspired by the Norman Conquest. Odo, Bishop of Bayeux, is a strong
       candidate for patron of the *CR*. *Il est escrit es cartres e es brefs* (v. 1682)
       recalls the terminology of the Anglo-Norman Chancery. Possible
       Norman origin of the *CR*. rev: Cigada, *SF*, V (1961), 121.

575   Bender, Karl-Heinz. "Les Métamorphoses de la royauté de
       Ch dans les premières épopées franco-italiennes." *CN*, XXI

(1961), 164-74.

Feudal concerns no longer dominate the Trial of Ganelon in the two Venice MSS of the *CR*, and as a result Ch's political and moral portrait improves.

576   Richthofen, Erich von. "Espíritu hispánico en una forma galorromana (I). Problemas épicos pendientes y sugerencias." *Boletín de Filología* (Chile), XII (1960), 5-49; XIII (1961), 5-31. Revised version in *Nuevos estudios*, pp. 147-215.

Ganelon is connected with García Ordóñez de Grañón, Baligant with Yúsuf.

577   Constantinescu, Nicolae. "Aspecte ale reflectării societății feudale în *Cîntecul lui Roland* [Aspects of feudal society in the *CR*]." *Studii*, XVI (1963), 565-89. Résumés in Russian and French, pp. 587-9.

The *CR* is of popular origin and reflects the ideals of the *bachelier* class. Bédier represents the bourgeois tradition of historiography.

578   Heisig, Karl. "Das *Rolandslied* und Byzanz." *Festschrift Rheinfelder*, pp. 161-78.

Ch is modeled on the ideal of the Byzantine prince, and *Romanie* in vv. 2326 and 3094 refers to the Byzantine Empire. rev: Müller, *ZFSL*, LXXV (1965), 78-9.

579   Ross, D.J.A. "L'Originalité de 'Turoldus': Le maniement de la lance." *CCM*, VI (1963), 127-38.

The technique of lance warfare found in *O* proves that its narrative of the Battle of Roncevaux dates from the last third of the eleventh c. at the earliest, and was the work of a *remanieur*.

580   Waltz, Matthias. *Rolandslied, Wilhelmslied, Alexiuslied: Zur Struktur und geschichtlichen Bedeutung.* (Studia Romanica, IX) Heidelberg: Carl Winter Verlag, 1965.

Emphasizes the values of chivalry, sense of collectivity, and conflict between the needs of the group and those of the individual. The *CR* does not reflect the society of its age, but is rather an interpretation of history based on the categories of good and evil. rev: Konrad, *Welt und Wort*, XXI (1966), 311; Whitehead, *FS*, XX (1966), 388-9; Burger, *MAe*, XXXV (1966), 240-8; De Cesare, *SF*, X (1966), 528; Sckommodau, *Archiv*, CCIV (1967), 148-50; Duby, *CCM*, X (1967), 483-4; Worthington, *RPh*, XXII (1968-9), 329-33; Payen, *MA*, LXXV (1969), 323-30; Segre, *ZRP*, LXXXVII (1971), 414-19.

581   Bender, Karl-Heinz. *König und Vasall: Untersuchungen zur Chanson de Geste des 12. Jahrhunderts.* (Studia Romanica, XIII) Heidelberg: Carl Winter Verlag, 1967.

Ch's situation reflects those of Henry I or Philip I, depending on the date one assigns to *O*. rev: Jodogne, *SF*, XII (1968), 329; Schon, *RF*, LXXX (1968), 495-7; Schulze, *Poetica*, II (1968), 275-9; Mauguit, *MR*, XX (1970), no. 4, pp. 134-7; Hackett, *RPh*, XXIV (1970-1), 228-30.

581A Satō, Teruo. "Hesuchingusu no arasoi to *Rōran no uta* [The battle of Hastings and the *CR*]." *Nihon Bungaku no Rekishi Geppō*, V (1967), 1-4.

Discusses the relation between *jongleur* and warrior, citing the *CR*, the *Chanson de Guillaume*, and *Raoul de Cambrai*.

582 Köhler, Erich. *Conseil des barons und jugement des barons: Epische Fatalität und Feudalrecht im altfranzösischen Rolandslied.* (Sitzungsberichte der Heidelberger Akademie der Wissenschaften, Philosophisch-historische Klasse, 1968, IV) Heidelberg: Carl Winter Verlag, 1968.

Only the barons sitting for *judicium* had the right to dictate to the king. In presenting the choice of the ambassador and of the leader of the rearguard as selections of the *consilium*, the *R* poet combines the two functions. The enmity between Ganelon and R may derive in part from Ganelon's position as a Count of the March, historically a figure in rebellious relationship to the king and his *maisnee*, here the Twelve Peers. rev: Hirdt, *SF*, XIII (1969), 520; Ross, *MLR*, LXV (1970), 418-19; Spoor, *Het Franse Boek*, XL (1970), 185-90; Schulze, *Poetica*, III (1970), 632-7; Whitehead, *FS*, XXV (1971), 314; Hackett, *RPh*, XXIV (1970-1), 556-7; Bender, *RF*, LXXXV (1973), 593-5.

583 Bender, Karl-Heinz. "Un Aspect de la stylisation épique: L'exclusivisme de la haute noblesse dans les chansons de geste du XIIe siècle." *Heidelberg Colloquium*, pp. 95-105.

While only the lowest level of nobility carried out its feudal obligations faithfully in the eleventh c., in the poem the highest nobles do so, which results in an idealized portrait.

584 Nichols, Stephen G., Jr. "The Interaction of Life and Literature in the *Peregrinationes ad Loca Sancta* and the *Chansons de Geste*." *Speculum*, XLIV (1969), 51-77.

Literary perceptions of an historical event were based on a continually evolving idea of the event. *O* and *V4* considered.

585 Villaneau, François. "Ch et R, ou la naissance d'un mythe." *Bulletin de la Société de Mythologie Française*, LXXIV (1969), 47-58.

Links *O* with the family of Henry Plantagenet, dating the version at around 1173 (thus ignoring philological and paleographic evidence).

Conjectures AOI as *adsonant omnia instrumenta*.

586 ——. "Ch et R, ou la genèse d'un mythe." *Bulletin de la Société d'Etudes Folkloriques du Centre-Ouest*, 1970, pp. 410-23; 1971, pp. 1-9.
Substantially the same as the preceding.

587 Poncet, Jean. "La *CR* à la lumière de l'histoire: Vérité de Baligant." *Revue de l'Occident Musulman et de la Méditerranée*, VIII (1970), 125-39.
Baligant is a combination of the two sons of Ali Ghāniya, the Ben Ali Ghāniya, lieutenants of the Almoravid sultan Ali ibn Yusuf. Other identifications of a similar nature. rev: Lecoy, *Romania*, XCIII (1972), 288; Di Stefano, *SF*, XVII (1973), 110.

588 Moorman, Charles. "The *Song of Roland.*" *King and Captains: Variations on a Heroic Theme.* Lexington: Univ. Press of Kentucky, 1971. Pp. 87-108.
Siding with neotraditionalism, C.M. examines feudal ideals in the *CR*, particularly the contrast between personal loyalties and national concerns. rev: Henn, *MLR*, LXVIII (1973), 141-2.

589 Kloocke, Kurt. "Kreuzzugsideologie und *Chansons de Geste.*" *Beiträge zur vergleichenden Literaturgeschichte: Festschrift für Kurt Wais zum 65. Geburtstag.* Edited by Johannes Hösle. Tübingen: Niemeyer, 1972. Pp. 1-18.
The *CR* is influenced by the ideology of the First Crusade and derives from a knightly rather than a clerical milieu.

See also 93, 290, 368, 385, 390, 402, 406, 431, 509, 557, 574.

ICONOGRAPHY

Among medieval heroes, none except Alexander inspired medieval artists more than did R.

590 Azevedo, António de. "Mais um passo da *CR* no românico português." *Bracara Augusta*, VIII (1957), 233-8.
Scenes on a capital in the Romanesque church at Rio Mau in N.W. Portugal represent R's death and Ch's search for the bodies.

591 Siebs, Benno Edie. "Stal-Roland-Rosengarten: Zur magischen Bedeutung der Gerichtsstätten." *ZSRG*, LXXVI (1959), 246-66.
Reviews the various etymologies proposed for "Roland" as a designation of the statues symbolizing law and found in German marketplaces. Favors *rauhes Land*, supposedly a survival from a time when justice was

rendered in an uncultivated field.

592 Gathen, Antonius David. *Rolande als Rechtssymbole: Der archäologische Bestand und seine rechtshistorische Deutung.* (Neue Kölner Rechtswissenschaftliche Abhandlungen, XIV) Berlin: De Gruyter, 1960.
The statues symbolized Law rather than any particular juridical concept or type of procedure. A.D.G. traces the view of Ch as a patron of law and sketches the political circumstances under the impetus of which the statues may have been erected. A catalogue provides descriptions, dates, and a bibliography for each statue, including those now destroyed.

593 Lejeune, Rita. "Trois épisodes de la *CR* sur un linteau de la Cathédrale d'Angoulême." *CRAIBL*, 1961, pp. 381-99.
The lintel contains episodes which show the influence of a *CR* in the Oxford tradition, and date from around 1120.

594 ——. "Le Linteau d'Angoulême et la *CR*." *Romania*, LXXXII (1961), 1-26.
The three episodes on the lintel can be identified as the combat of Turpin with Abisme, the battle between R and Marsile, and the retreat of Marsile to Saragossa. rev: Salet, *Bulletin Monumental*, CXX (1962), 218-20.

595 ——. "R et Olivier au portail du Dôme de Vérone." *CN*, XXI (1961), 229-45.
The statues represent R and Oliver. The inscription DURINDARDA is authentic.

596 Stiennon, Jacques. "Le Pseudo-R de Vercelli: Essai d'interprétation d'une mosaïque médiévale." *CN*, XXI (1961), 246-58.
A mosaic in the church of Santa Maria Maggiore in Vercelli does not represent R.

597 Mitić, Ilija. "Die Rolandsäule in Ragusa (Dubrovnik)." *Z SRG* LXXXII (1965), 306-16.
A local legend has R defending the city against Saracen pirates in the year 783; the pillar was erected in 1419.

598 Dodwell, Charles R. "The Bayeux Tapestry and the French Secular Epic." *The Burlington Magazine*, CVIII (1966), 549-60.
Analogies between the depictions on the Tapestry and the purpose, motivation, themes, characterization, and narrative technique of the *chanson de geste.*

599 Lejeune, Rita, and Jacques Stiennon. *La Légende de R dans*

l'art du moyen âge. 2 vols. Paris: Editions Sequoia; Brussels: Arcade, 1966. German ed.: *Die Rolandssage in der mittel- alterlichen Kunst.* Translated by Barbara Ronge. Brussels: Arcade, 1966. English: *The Legend of Roland in the Middle Ages.* Translated by Christine Trollope. New York: Phaidon, 1971.

A monumental study of the iconography of R from the early twelfth c. into the sixteenth, in arts both major and minor. All aspects of the legend are treated, including Ch's Sin, R's childhood, scenes from the *Pseudo-Turpin Chronicle* and Konrad's *Ruolantes Liet*, Baldwin's pre- sence at Roncevaux, and scenes from *chansons de geste* other than the *CR*. In general, the medieval representations, some of which are master- works, have deviated little from the details furnished by literary texts. R's combat with the giant Ferragut is shown to be a theme older than the *Pseudo-Turpin Chronicle*, the text in which it first appears. Illustra- tions in color in vol. I, in black-and-white in vol. II which consists entirely of plates. rev: Zumthor, *Het Franse Boek*, XXXVI (1966), 200-1; Durliat, *AMi*, LXXVIII (1966), 559-61; Delcourt, *RBPH*, XLIV (1966), 1032-3; Labande-Mailfert, *CCM*, IX (1966), 417-21; Higounet, *Revue Historique du Département de la Gironde*, XV (1966), 207-9; Lacarra, *Estudios de Edad Media de la Corona de Aragón*, VIII (1967), 720-1; Lecoy, *Romania*, LXXXVIII (1967), 418-22; Bossuat, *Journal des Savants*, 1967, pp. 180-2; Köhler, *GRM*, XVIII (1968), 214-15; Di Stefano, *SF*, XII (1968), 119; Lhéritier, *BBF*, XIII (1968), 46-7; Legge, *FS*, XXII (1968), 133; McCulloch, *Speculum*, XLIII (1968), 176-80; Le Gentil, *MA*, LXXIV (1968), 87-99; Ross, *MAe*, XXXVII (1968), 46-65 (rev: Mann, *SF*, XIII [1969], 114); Green, *MLR*, LXIII (1968), 926-9; Peckham, *RR*, LX (1969), 186-8. *TLS*, March 3, 1972, 240 (rev. of English translation).

600   Lejeune, Rita. "Turold dans la tapisserie de Bayeux." *Mélanges Crozet*, vol. I, pp. 419-25.

Turold, one of Duke William's ambassadors in the Tapestry, has a *jongleur* with him.

601   Lejeune, Rita, and Jacques Stiennon. "Le Héros R 'neveu de Ch' dans l'iconographie médiévale." *Karl der Grosse*, IV: *Das Nachleben*. Düsseldorf: Schwann, 1967. Pp. 215-28.

Largely a summation of the findings of 599. Illustrations.

602   Siebs, Benno Eide. "Jedute und R." *ZSRG*, LXXXIV (1967), 293-310.

The name R associated with statues does not originally designate the hero, but is rather to be linked with Germanic roots signifying untamed strength.

603   Lejeune, Rita. "La Légende de R dans l'art italien du moyen

âge." *La poesia epica*, pp. 299-314.

Transformations of R's legend in medieval Italian art.

604   Short, Ian. "Le Pape Calixte II, Ch et les fresques de Santa Maria in Cosmedin." *CCM,* XIII (1970), 229-38.

The frescoes have nothing to do with either Ch or Calixtus, contrary to the hypothesis of Lejeune and Stiennon (599).

605   D'Oldenico, G. Donna. "L'architrave della Collegiata di Domo e la narrativa medioevale lungo la via 'francisca' dell' Ossola." *Oscellana*, I (1971), 23-32.

The relief (middle twelfth c.) represents Ch in bed, watched over by the angel Gabriel.

606   Ratkowska, Paulina. "Smierć Aude'y: Przyczynek do badán nad pewnym wątkiem literackim w ikonografii świeckiej XIV wieku [The death of Alda: Contribution to research on a literary motif in fourteenth-c. lay iconography]." *Biuletyn Historii Sztuki* (Warsaw), XXXIV (1972), 235-51. French summary, pp. 250-1.

On the miniature depicting Alda's death on folio 623 of the Berlin MS. of Stricker's *Karl der Grosse*. Discussion of the ideals presented in Alda's death scene. Illustrations.

607   D'Oldenico, G. Donna. "Chi fu il committente dell'architrave della Chiesa Collegiata di Domodossola?" *Oscellana*, III (1973), 37.

Count Guido di Biandrate, who took part in the crusade of 1148, commissioned the work.

608   Gasca Queirazza, Giuliano. "La Figuration rolandienne de l'architrave de Domodossola." *Congrès d'Aix*, pp. 205-19.

The relief shows Ch's third dream. Also represented are Blancandrin, the Saracen hostages, and perhaps R.

See also 622.

LATER DEVELOPMENT

The R legend was taken up by later poets, especially in Spain and Italy, and is still the subject of four living traditions: the puppet theater of Sicily, the Faroese ballad, the pan-Hispanic *romance*, and the oral poetry of northwest Brazil.

609   Horrent, Jules. *La CR dans les littératures française et espagnole au moyen âge.* (Bibl. de la Fac. de Philosophie et

Lettres de l'Univ. de Liège, CXX) Paris: Société d'Edition "Les Belles Lettres", 1951.

Very important study, treating the relationship between various literary versions of the R legend, including the *Pseudo-Turpin Chronicle* and texts devoted to Galien, son of Oliver, and to the Spanish anti-R, Bernardo del Carpio. The original *CR* was written by a cleric between the end of the tenth c. and 1050. The Episode of Baligant was added around the time of the First Crusade. Many fine literary and historical observations. Bibliography, pp. 11-23.

610   —. "Sur les *romances* carolingiens de Roncevaux." *LR*, IX (1955), 161-76.

Traces the hostility of the Spanish *romancistas* toward R, Oliver, and Ch, examining in particular "La fuga del rey Marsín", "Por muchas partes herido sale el viejo Carlomagno", the *romances* of Bernardo del Carpio, don Beltrán, Guarinos, and Alda, and learned texts of the sixteenth c.

611   —. "Chroniques espagnoles et chansons de geste, III: Nouvelles remarques sur l'*Historia Silense*." *MA*, LXII (1956), 279-99.

The Monk of Silos is reacting against the Carolingian historiographic tradition rather than against the assertions of epic poets. rev: De Cesare, *SF*, I (1957), 287. See also 569.

612   —. "Sur deux témoignages espagnols de la *CR*." *BH*, LVIII (1956), 48-50.

A learned and clerical reaction to the legend of R results in pejorative mentions in the *Chronica Adefonsi Imperatoris* (*ca* 1152) and the *Vida de San Millán* (early thirteenth c.). rev: Groult, *LR*, XI (1957), 300.

613   Li Gotti, Ettore. "Roncisvalle nell'Opera dei pupi e la leggenda rolandiana nell'epoca normanna in Sicilia." *Coloquios de Roncesvalles*, pp. 277-300.

The tradition of puppet theater with R as its subject does not descend directly from the medieval *jongleresque* tradition.

614   Monteverdi, Angelo. "Rinaldo di Montalbano e Bernardo del Carpio a Roncisvalle." *Coloquios de Roncesvalles*, pp. 263-76.

Pulci's representation of Renaut de Montauban at Roncevaux in the *Morgante* probably derives from the *Pseudo-Turpin Chronicle*. Parallels between the legend of Bernardo del Carpio and the fourteenth-c. Italian *Berte et Milon* possibly explained by a common French source.

615   —. "A proposito delle fonti dell'*Orlando furioso*." *CN*, XXI (1961), 258-67.

Ariosto did not know *V4* or *V7*, although he could well have had access to them.

616   ——· "Lipadusa e Roncisvalle." *LI*, XIII (1961), 401-9.
Echoes of the *CR* in *Orlando furioso.*

617   Roncaglia, Aurelio. *"Les quatre eschieles de Rollant."* *CN*, XXI (1961), 191-205.
The *Roman de Thèbes* mentions (v. 8826) that R commanded *quatre eschieles* in the rearguard, a detail known only to the *Entrée d'Espagne*, whose ultimate source appears to be the lost *Prise de Nobles.*

618   Zaddy, Zara P. "Chrétien de Troyes and the Epic Tradition." *CN*, XXI (1961), 71-82.
Analogies between the *CR* and the romances of Chrétien, especially *Erec et Enide.*

619   Boni, Marco. "La *CR* e le *Canzoni di re Enzio.*" *Studi per il centenario della nascità di Giovanni Pascoli.* Bologna: Commissione per i Testi di Lingua, 1962. Vol. II, pp. 189-98.
Also printed in *Convivium*, XXX (1962), 40-6.
Influence of the *CR* on Pascoli.

620   Câmara Cascudo, Luís da. "R no Brasil." *Ocidente*, LXII (1962), 70-5. Tr. by Jean-Marie d'Heur, "R au Brésil." *MR*, XII.(1962), 70-6.
The legend of R is alive in the oral poetry of northwest Brazil, where it was introduced in the nineteenth c.

621   Heur, Jean-Marie d'. "R au Brésil: Note additionnelle." *MR*, XIII (1963), 85-95.

622   ——. "R au Portugal et aussi en Espagne, dans l'art et dans la littérature: deux ou trois problèmes iconographiques." *Hommage à Maurice Delbouille*, pp. 123-46.

623   Ruggieri, Ruggero M. "Il titolo e la protasi dell'*Entrée d'Espagne* e dei *Fatti di Spagna* in rapporto alla materia della *CR*." *Mélanges Delbouille*, vol. II, pp. 615-33.
Themes of the Franco-Italian and Italian works related to *O* and to *Roncesvalles*, the *Pseudo-Turpin Chronicle*, and *Ronsasvals.* rev: D'Heur, *MR*, XX (1970), 118.

624   Roldán Loris, Juana. *La huella histórico-literaria de Roldán en los textos españoles de la Edad Media y en los romances.* Madrid: Ediciones Cultura Hispánica, 1972. Originally a thesis: Univ. of Southern California, 1968. *DAI*, XXIX

(1968-9), 1233-4A.

625   MacLean, Doris G. "*La belle Aude* Comes to Life in the
Spanish Ballad." *Proceedings of the Pacific Northwest
Conference on Foreign Languages.* Victoria, British
Columbia: Univ. of Victoria, Vol. XX (1969), pp. 8-11.
General treatment.

626   Cantel, Raymond. "La persistencia de los temas medievales
de Europa en la literatura popular del Nordeste brasileño."
Actas del III Congreso Internacional de Hispanistas, edited by
Carlos H. Magis. Mexico City: Colegio de México, 1970. Pp.
175-85.
Characteristics of the Carolingian legends which descend from the
*História do Imperador Carlos Magno e dos doze Pares de França traduzi-
da do castelhano por Jerónimo Moreira de Carvalho.*

627   Celletti, Maria Chiara. "Santi Rolando, Olivero e compagni."
Bibliotheca sanctorum. Rome: Istituto Giovanni XXIII della
Pontifica Università Lateranense, 1962-70. Vol. XI (1968),
pp. 303-6.
Summary of the legend of R, who was venerated as a saint as early as
the thirteenth c.

628   Ciarambino, Geraldo C. A. "Carlomagno, Gano e Orlando in
alcuni romanzi italiani del XIV e del XV secolo." Thesis:
Columbia, 1973. *DAI,* XXXV (1974-5), 1041-2A. *Olifant,*
II (1974-5), 144-6.

See also 36, 541, 542, 557.

INDEX OF SCHOLARS AND TRANSLATORS

* * *

References are to item numbers, unless preceded by 'p.'

QUEEN MARY
COLLEGE
LIBRARY